By Ken Blanchard

HIGH FIVE! *(with Sheldon Bowles), 2001*

MANAGEMENT OF ORGANIZATIONAL BEHAVIOR: UTILIZING HUMAN RESOURCES *(with Paul Hersey), 8th Edition, 2000*

BIG BUCKS! *(with Sheldon Bowles), 2000*

LEADERSHIP BY THE BOOK, *(with Bill Hybels and Phil Hodges), 1999*

THE HEART OF A LEADER, *1999*

GUNG HO! *(with Sheldon Bowles), 1998*

RAVING FANS: A REVOLUTIONARY APPROACH TO CUSTOMER SERVICE, *(with Sheldon Bowles), 1993*

MANAGEMENT BY VALUES *(with Michael O'Connor), 1997*

MISSION POSSIBLE *(with Terry Waghorn), 1996*

EMPOWERMENT TAKES MORE THAN A MINUTE *(with John P. Carlos and Alan Randolph), 1996*

EVERYONE'S A COACH *(with Dan Shula), 1995*

WE ARE THE BELOVED, *1994*

PLAYING THE GREAT GAME OF GOLF: MAKING EVERY *MINUTE* COUNT, *1992*

THE ONE MINUTE MANAGER® BUILDS HIGH PERFORMING TEAMS *(with Don Carew and Eunice Parisi-Carew), 1990*

THE ONE MINUTE MANAGER® MEETS THE MONKEY *(with William Oncken, Jr., and Hal Burrows), 1989*

THE POWER OF ETHICAL MANAGEMENT *(with Norman Vincent Peale), 1988*

THE ONE MINUTE MANAGER® GETS FIT *(with D. W. Edington and Marjorie Blanchard), 1986*

LEADERSHIP AND THE ONE MINUTE MANAGER® *(with Patricia Zigarmi and Drea Zigarmi), 1985*

ORGANIZATIONAL CHANGE THROUGH EFFECTIVE LEADERSHIP *(with Robert H. Guest and Paul Hersey), 2nd Edition, 1985*

PUTTING THE ONE MINUTE MANAGER® TO WORK *(with Robert Lorber), 1984*

THE ONE MINUTE MANAGER® *(with Spencer Johnson), 1982*

THE FAMILY GAME: A SITUATIONAL APPROACH TO EFFECTIVE PARENTING *(with Paul Hersey), 1979*

By Jim Ballard

WHAT'S THE RUSH? *1999*

Whale Done!

The Power of Positive Relationships

Ken Blanchard,

Thad Lacinak,

Chuck Tompkins,

and Jim Ballard

THE FREE PRESS

New York   London   Toronto   Sydney   Singapore

THE FREE PRESS
A Division of Simon & Schuster, Inc.
1230 Avenue of the Americas
New York, NY 10020

THE FREE PRESS and colophon are trademarks
of Simon & Schuster, Inc.

For information regarding special discounts for bulk purchases,
please contact Simon & Schuster Special Sales:
1-800-456-6798 or business@simonandschuster.com

Designed by Lisa Chovnick

Manufactured in the United States of America

1   3   5   7   9   10   8   6   4   2

Library of Congress Cataloging-in-Publication Data is available

ISBN 0-7432-3538-X

We dedicate this book to our unsung heroes—the many committed individuals who have been quietly and faithfully going about the business of catching people they know and love doing things right. After reading this book, we hope the list of people who fall under that dedication will include you.

WHALE DONE, friends!

 Introduction

by Ken Blanchard

In 1976, when my family and I came to San Diego on sabbatical from the University of Massachusetts in Amherst, one of the first places we visited was SeaWorld. Everyone we talked to urged us to see the Shamu killer-whale show. Since I was aware that killer whales are considered the most feared predators in the ocean, I didn't know what to expect. Would we just be watching them swim around? What a surprise when we entered Shamu Stadium and the show began! Before a minute had gone by, all of us were raving fans. As I watched these incredible creatures leap and dive, and even carry their trainers on their backs, I found myself fascinated. How had they been trained to perform such feats, and with such evident delight?

For years I had been talking and writing about the power of positive relationships and the need to catch people doing things right in order to develop productive work and home environments. And yet I'd become discouraged to see that the very opposite was occurring in most organizations and homes: catching people doing things wrong seemed to be the rule. I was firmly convinced that punishment was harmful in human relationships, and I realized instinctively that it wouldn't be a smart move with killer whales. That belief was borne out when I took a group of our trainers and clients on a behind-the-scenes tour of the Shamu show, and met Chuck Tompkins, head trainer at the Orlando SeaWorld. Chuck and I, recognizing each other as soul mates, made an agreement: he would teach me about whale training and I would teach him about people training. In the process we found we were teaching the same things!

Yet we also had important concepts to learn from one another. I was particularly fascinated by the ability of SeaWorld trainers to use *redirection*. Upon encountering any undesirable behaviors on the whales' part, they would immediately refocus those energies elsewhere. That very simple but powerful strategy permits the trainers to set up new situations to catch the whales doing something right. Everybody knows that accentuating the positive works best. But what do you do when somebody does something that has a negative impact? That's where Chuck and the SeaWorld trainers opened my eyes. Instead of focusing energy, as most of us do, on what went wrong, they redirect that energy toward a positive outcome. When Chuck and I realized that the combination of redirection and accentuating the positive could make a major difference in work and family relationships, we began talking about writing a book together that would show how to apply these concepts.

That project remained a dream for several years until Chuck introduced me to his boss, colleague, and friend, Thad Lacinak. Now we had three dreamers determined to make it happen. A little later I invited Jim Ballard, an old friend, colleague, and writing partner, to join forces with us. With that critical mass, *WHALE DONE!* began to take shape. I am thrilled with this book and think it might be the most important book I have ever written.

 Chapter One

How do they *do* that?

A collective gasp rose from a crowd of over three thousand spectators as they thrilled to the amazing performances of leaping killer whales. It was another show in Shamu Stadium at SeaWorld. All eyes in the grandstand were glued to the huge animals and their trainers, so no one noticed the wide range of emotions reflected in the face of a man in khakis and a blue shirt who sat in their midst. Each time the crowd exploded in applause and cheers as the animals performed one of their spectacular feats, the man's eyes would sparkle with surprise and delight. At other times his face would cloud over and his eyes assume a faraway look.

Wes Kingsley had come to Orlando to attend a business conference. Since the schedule left room for conferees to relax, play golf, or visit one of the area's attractions, he had decided that a visit to the world-famous marine zoological park would help him forget his troubles for a time.

He was glad he had made that decision. Earlier, along with throngs of other people eagerly crowding the huge stadium, he had taken his seat above the blue waters of the large main pool. Following a welcome and a review of safety rules by an animal trainer, a mysterious fog had begun to shroud the surface of the pool. From behind and above them, the crowd heard the scream of a fish eagle. The mighty bird suddenly swooped over their heads, dove toward the pool, and took a lure from the misty waters. As it flew away, huge black dorsal fins broke the surface, and onlookers caught their breath when they saw monstrous black shapes circling deep in the pool. A wet-suit-clad trainer came through the mists paddling a kayak, to be instantly surrounded by the fins of enormous killer whales.

Following this dramatic opening, the crowd witnessed a series of astonishing acrobatic leaps and dives by a trio of whales—a 10,000-pound male and two 5,000-pound females. These marine mammals, among the most feared predators in the ocean, waved their pectoral fins to the audience, allowed trainers to "surf" the pool by balancing on their back, and with sweeps of their great tails splashed the first ten rows of spectators with cold water. The roars of laughter, the oohs and aahs, and the thunderous applause attested to the crowd's enjoyment.

Wes Kingsley also found himself entranced by the spectacle unfolding before him. By the finale, when the three finny costars hiked their gleaming black-backed and white-bellied bodies up onto a raised section of the pool to take some well-deserved bows, he had scribbled several entries in a small notebook.

As people exited the stadium, scores of them were still dripping from the soaking they'd happily received sitting in the "splash zone" of the first ten rows. Despite this—or perhaps because of it—their faces sparkled with smiles. Still in his seat in an upper row of the emptying stands, Wes Kingsley remained staring down into the pool. Its blue depths, recently awash with great waves but now still, seemed to echo his mood.

After the crowd had left and the place was quiet, an underwater gate opened and a giant black form moved into the pool and began circling it. A trainer came through a door and strolled out onto the lip of the pool, and the huge killer whale immediately swam over to him. "Nice going, big guy," he said, stroking its head. "Enjoy your playtime. You earned it." As the trainer rose and walked along the pool's edge, the whale moved with him. It seemed to be trying to stay as close to him as possible.

The blue-shirted man in the stands shook his head and thought to himself, *You'd think that after doing a whole show that whale would hoard its free time. But what does it want to do? Play with the trainer!* A question was forming in the man's mind, a need to know that had been building up in him ever since the start of the show. He had an impulse to go down there and ask the trainer that question, but fear of embarrassment held him back. Then suddenly he got up off the bench and quickly descended the stairs.

"Excuse me," Wes called as he reached the deck of the pool and started toward the trainer.

The trainer looked up in surprise. Then he gestured toward a door. "Sir, the exit is over there."

"I know. But I need to ask you something." As Wes approached, it was evident that he was not ready to take no for an answer.

"Sure," the trainer said. "What do you want to know?"

Pulling a wallet from his pocket, Wes offered two fifty-dollar bills to the trainer. "I'm willing to pay you for the information. What I want to know is probably what everyone who sees the show wonders: What's your secret? How do you trick these animals into performing for you? Do you starve them?"

The man in the wet suit controlled an impulse to

react angrily to his visitor's impertinent attitude. Patiently and quietly he said, "We don't trick them, and we don't starve them. And you can keep your money."

"Well then, what is it? What *do* you do?" Wes demanded. But after a long silence from the other, Wes's manner softened. Realizing he had given offense, he put his money away. "Sorry," he said, holding out his hand. "I'm Wes Kingsley. I don't mean to bother you with this, but I really have to know how you get such a tremendous performance from these animals."

"Dave Yardley," said the trainer as they shook hands. "I'm in charge of the animal training here, so I guess you might say you've come to the right place. The answer to your question is that we have teachers. Would you like to meet one of them?"

Kingsley looked around to see if they were being joined by someone else. When he looked back, Yardley was pointing to the whale. "This is one of our teachers. His name's Shamu. He and all the other whales here at SeaWorld taught us all we know about working with these wonderful animals."

Wes squinted warily. "Come on. You mean to say you've been trained by an *animal?* I thought it was the other way around."

Dave shook his head. "Shamu is one of the world's largest killer whales living in a zoological park. As far as who trains whom, let me put it this way. When you're dealing with an eleven-thousand-pound animal who doesn't speak English, you do a lot of learning."

Wes glanced down at the rows of enormous, two-inch-long teeth in Shamu's enormous mouth. "I think the only thing he would teach me is to stay on his good side."

"There's plenty of data to back that up," Dave said. "Killer whales are the most feared predators in the ocean. They can kill and eat anything in sight."

"I guess if he's not learning his lessons, you don't make him go and stand in the corner," Wes ventured.

"That's exactly right. One thing we learned quickly was that it doesn't make much sense to punish a killer whale and then ask a trainer to get in the water with him."

"Not unless you want your career shortened!" Wes exclaimed. Then, recalling the prodigious leaps Shamu had performed in the show, he added, "It's hard to believe a creature that size could get ten feet out of the water on its own. How *do* you get him to perform so well?"

"Let's just say it didn't happen overnight," said Dave. "Shamu taught us patience."

"How so?"

"Shamu wasn't about to do anything for me or any

other trainer until he trusted us. As I worked with him, it became clear that I couldn't train him until he was convinced of my intentions. Whenever we get a new whale, we don't attempt to do any training for some time. All we do is make sure they're not hungry; then we jump in the water and play with them, until we convince them."

"Convince them of what?"

"That we mean them no harm."

Wes said, "You mean you want them to trust you."

"You're right. That's the key principle we use in working with all our animals."

Wes took out his notebook and pen and began to write.

"Are you writing an article?" Dave asked. "Or doing research?"

Wes Kingsley smiled grimly. "I guess you'd call it research of a personal nature. I've got to learn some new things myself or else . . ."

Dave Yardley waited and watched. *It's hard for this guy to trust anybody,* he thought. *That's what his bluster act is about.*

After a long pause, Wes spoke, avoiding eye contact with the trainer. "I live near Atlanta and work for a big industrial-supply outfit. I came to Florida to get away for a few days, using a business conference as the excuse. But over there at the hotel with my manager buddies, all I could think of was how I don't want to go back home to face the same old problems."

Dave was listening with evident interest.

"For a long time I've been having a hard time getting my people at work to perform well," Wes continued, then grinned. "Not to mention getting my kids at home to pitch in around the house and do better at school. When I was complaining to a friend of mine about it, he had a nice way of suggesting that since I was having management problems both at work and at home, we might look for the common denominator."

"What was that?" Dave asked.

"My friend said, 'Did you ever notice, when your life isn't working, *who's always around?*' "

Both men chuckled. "I know I'm not managing effectively," Wes went on, "and I might be about to lose my job. Frankly, I'm getting a little desperate."

Dave was aware of Wes's anxious, almost pleading tone of voice and said, "Let me take you on a little backstage tour. Then we can talk more about this."

Dave led Wes through a gate and over to a training pool where a few feet away the huge black backs and fins of two killer whales were gliding through the clear blue water. Their beautiful bodies exuded an air of calmness, and at the same time the promise of explosive power. As the two men walked from one holding pool to another, the trainer identified each whale by name and supplied interesting anecdotes about them.

"It takes a long time to build trust and friendship with each of the whales," Dave said. "That trust and friendship is the basis of everything you just saw in the show. These animals are not so different from people. They'll show you when they don't like how you're treating them. You're a businessman, so you know that the whole game these days is satisfying the customer—and a key ingredient of that is satisfying your own people. When our killer whales completely lose their fear of us, the positive vibes between them and us are transferred to the audience."

"That's true," said Wes emphatically. "The show creates a lot of happiness in the audience. I could see it on people's faces when they left the stadium. Half of them were soaking wet, yet there were big smiles on their faces."

"You can see it in the whales, too," Dave said, "They all crowd up to the gate when the show is starting. It's plain they want to be in it. They know it's going to be a positive experience."

"Okay, I've got the principle. But what do you actually *do* with the whales to build that trust?"

"You might want to write this down." Dave smiled. "We . . .

Accentuate the positive.

"Hm," Wes mused. "I think there's an old song about that." He took out his notebook and began writing again. "So, it goes: *Build trust . . . Accentuate the positive*. Is that right?"

"Right. We accentuate the positive, not the negative. We pay a lot of attention when the animal does what we ask him to do and performs a task correctly."

"That sounds fine," Wes said insistently. "But what about when he *doesn't* do it, or does it *in*correctly?"

"We ignore what he did wrong and immediately redirect his behavior elsewhere."

Wes stopped writing and looked up, obviously bothered. "What exactly do you mean by *ignore?*"

"I mean—"

"If one of my people screws up," Wes interrupted, his voice agitated, "I can't afford to just look the other way. If one of my kids doesn't do her homework, or picks on her sister, my wife and I are certainly not going to *ignore* it!'"

"Then I'm guessing," Dave said quietly, "that when people in your shop or your kids at home do something that displeases you, you pay lots of attention to it."

"Darn right I do."

"You probably tell them you didn't like what they did. And you warn them about doing it again."

"Hey," Wes exploded defensively. "Isn't that my job as a manager? Isn't that what any responsible parent does?"

The trainer shrugged. "*You* say it is. But I wonder, is that the way to build a trusting environment at the office or at home?"

That caught Wes by surprise. "Come to think of it," he said, "I guess not. That's more like accentuating the negative."

Dave nodded. "An important concept to remember is that *the more attention you pay to a behavior, the more it will be repeated.* We've learned from the killer whales that when we *don't* pay a lot of attention to what they do wrong, but instead give *lots* of attention to what they do *right,* they do the right thing more often."

"So you're saying it's what you focus on that is the key."

"Exactly. We don't accentuate the positive just to get

the animals to perform, though. We do it because it's
the right thing to do. We treat our animals as individuals, each of which has unlimited capacities for develop-
ment and accomplishment. We make every effort to
persuade the animals to see us as their friends. After
friendship is established, we try to find out just where
we and the particular animal can meet on a basis of
mutual trust and understanding. We study its behavior
patterns to find out what it likes. Then we make everything in the training into a game, injecting easy lessons
that the animals learn almost without effort."

Wes was amazed. "You talk about these animals as if
they're superintelligent, as if they *want* to be friendly
and cooperate with humans."

"They do," Dave said. "But humans must do their
part. One of the most harmful practices in animal edu-
cation is the human habit of mentally limiting animals.
What the human thinks about an animal, and expects
from an animal, has a direct bearing on that animal's
response or lack of response."

"I've never heard these ideas applied to animals
before."

"That's because people in general look down on animals," Dave continued. "The conventional approach to
animal training is one in which a 'superior' being com-
pels an 'inferior' one to do what he or she wants done.

Animals can sense expectations with astonishing accuracy. They can 'live down' to human expectations just like people can. But you should never be surprised when an animal does what you ask, even when you ask the first time. These killer whales have taught us to always expect the impossible. This helps us more than it does the animal. If there is no response, that's a sign that we need more educating ourselves. Not the animal."

"I think most people don't accord their fellow humans, let alone their pets and animals, the kind of respect and understanding you're describing," Wes said. "*I* certainly haven't. No wonder these whales do an outstanding job! It would make a huge turnaround in my career as a manager, and as a husband and father, if I could begin to apply such a thoughtful, respectful philosophy in my relationships. It's a tall order, though."

"You'd better believe it!" Dave said emphatically.

Wes wrote down some more notes. Then he said, "I understand that what you focus on is the key. I still don't get the part about ignoring bad behavior."

Dave nodded. "When I say we ignore undesirable behavior, I don't mean we do nothing. You might have missed what I said about *redirecting.*"

"Redirecting, right," Wes murmured, writing another note. "Tell me more about that."

"It's all about energy management. It begins with controlling our own attention. A simple but very powerful rule to remember is, *if you don't want to encourage poor behavior, don't spend a lot of time on it.* Instead we rechannel the energy."

"Rechannel energy," Wes repeated slowly as he wrote down the phrase. "How do you do that?"

"It depends. If the thing we asked the animal to do is integral to the show, we simply direct his attention back to the original task we asked for and give him another chance to do it right. Other times we direct the animal's attention toward something else we want him to do, something he likes and can do well. In either case, following the redirection, we watch to see if we can catch him doing something right, so we can accentuate the positive and give him a treat."

"You mean something to eat?"

"Food certainly can be a treat," Dave said. "But we wanted to find other things he liked. Before I worked with him, Shamu had been taught on continuous food reinforcement. Whenever he did anything he was supposed to do, he got a fish. Now, can you see a certain drawback to that?"

"Sure. The only time he'd want to perform for you was when he was hungry. You'd have to keep him hungry all the time!"

"Exactly, and that wasn't a good idea for him or the trainer." Dave smiled. "We had to get him used to other positives, like rubbing his head. The whales like to be touched and rubbed. We wanted him to be very clear that we did not use punishment as a motivator, and also that there were other treats besides food."

"What you're telling me about varying the reward makes sense." Wes looked up from his notes. "But again, I'm trying to apply all this to my back-home situation. I'm thinking that, in a way, money may be to humans like food is to animals—it only provides the basics. If I want to influence the performance of my people using your method, I have to find other motivators besides money." Wes paused, then said, "It's hard to believe, but maybe you and Shamu are the ones to help me find some answers."

Dave smiled, seeing for the first time a likable, child-like spirit that had been hidden behind Wes's brash exterior. Dave turned suddenly and walked over to a nearby office building, reached inside an open window, and came away with a cell phone. Punching in a number, he said to Wes, "Excuse me. I have to make this call."

Annoyed, Wes walked off a few yards. His face had begun to freeze into its former mask of invulnerability. *I'm a fool,* he thought. *Who looks for answers to his relationship problems from a bunch of whales?* He glanced at his watch. If he hurried, he could still make it back to the hotel for the lunch meeting.

Dave spoke into the phone. "Anne Marie? Hi, it's Dave Yardley down at SeaWorld. How's it going?" There was a pause, then the trainer said, "Listen, my friend, I've got someone here who needs to talk with you. . . . Yeah, he's standing right here. His name is Wes Kingsley, and he's very interested to know how we train the animals, and whether these principles and techniques could be applied to relationships with people. He says he's particularly interested in applying them to business relationships."

Dave listened for a few moments. Then he said, "I know, isn't that something? And get this: he comes from Atlanta. So, shall I put him on the line?"

Somewhat embarrassed, Wes walked over to Dave, who was holding out the phone to him.

"Forgive me, Wes," Dave said. "I thought you could get some help from my friend, so I called her. Maybe you've heard of her. Her name is Anne Marie Butler. She's quite well-known as a business consultant. She writes books and travels all around the world leading business seminars on leadership and human motivation. She's based in Atlanta."

Wes felt a momentary panic. The name Anne Marie

Butler was indeed familiar to him. She was recognized as one of the top women executives in the country. As a young business-school grad she had started a clothing business and had in a few years built it to an internationally recognized fashion line. Her success in hiring and retaining top employees became legendary and led to her becoming an in-demand management consultant, the author of several best-selling books, and a star on the human relations speaking circuit. Wes had seen some of her books, but he had never read them. Feeling strange, he took the phone.

"Hello?"

"Hello, Wes," a friendly voice said. "This is Anne Marie Butler. I've known Dave for years, and I'm very happy to be talking with you. What can I do for you?"

"Well, uh . . . ," Wes stammered. "I've been talking to Dave here and trying to figure some ways I can use his animal-training techniques in my job as a manager."

Anne Marie laughed. "It wasn't too many years ago that I was right where you are, watching those whales perform and wondering, 'My gosh, how do they do that?' In my work as a management consultant, I'm always looking for ideas and strategies I can pass on to others that will help them get the best out of their people. When I got to know Dave and the other

trainers at SeaWorld, I felt they'd been heaven-sent.
And after I found out some of their animal-training
secrets, I started incorporating them into my
consulting, speeches, and books. More importantly, I
began to use them in my own relationships."

Dazed, Wes had the odd feeling that he was in the
right place at the right time. Anne Marie's repetition of
his own answer-to-a-prayer admission of moments
before struck him as dreamlike. "It's very good of you
to talk with me," he finally said. "Maybe you can
recommend some of your books where you've written
about these things."

"Better yet, why don't we get together? When are
you flying back to Atlanta?"

"On Friday."

"Well, it so happens I'm giving a convention speech
Monday morning at the downtown Hilton. Why don't
you sit in? We could have a talk afterwards."

"Really? That would be great!" Wes exclaimed.
"Thanks a lot." He handed the phone back to Dave.
After Dave had said good-bye to Anne Marie and hung
up, Wes blurted out, "I can't believe I'm going to meet
with Anne Marie Butler. I've really got to thank you,
Dave."

"My pleasure," the trainer said sincerely, and the two
men shook hands.

Wes flipped through the pages of his notebook, hurriedly reviewing what he had written. "Before I go, he said, "do you mind if I summarize some of the key points you've covered this morning?"

"Be my guest."

- Build trust.
- Accentuate the positive.
- When mistakes occur, redirect the energy.

"You've captured the real meat of it there, Wes," Dave said. Then he added, "Just remember, everything you see in the Shamu show is based on and driven by our positive relationships with the animals."

"Seriously," said Wes in a confidential tone, "don't you ever punish them?"

"Nope. There are times when they don't want to cooperate with us. Whales are just like humans. There are days when they get up on the wrong side of the pool. We've been known to stop the show when things just aren't working out, and we tell the audience that Shamu needs some time-out. As the other animals take over, Shamu goes to a backstage pool."

"Then what happens?"

"He rarely stays there long. These whales love to perform. And the more we accentuate the positive, the more they trust us and the better their performance."

"You know, it's odd, my coming here today," Wes said.

"How do you mean?" Dave asked.

"Well, I come to SeaWorld to get away from thinking about work, and find instead that I'm in management training."

"Strange as it may sound," Dave said, "that's what working with whales is all about."

Chapter Two

THE FOLLOWING MONDAY, Wes Kingsley drove to the downtown hotel where Anne Marie Butler would be speaking. Leaving his car with the valet, he entered the hotel and joined the large crowd milling about. He found a badge waiting for him at the receptionist's table and took a seat in the rear of the hall. When the place was filled, the moderator came to the podium and welcomed the crowd.

"Those of you who are familiar with Anne Marie Butler's work, or have heard her speak, know that we're in for a rare treat, and that the accent will be positive. Without further delay, please join me in welcoming one of the truly affirmative voices in business today—Anne Marie Butler." A round of applause broke out as an attractive, middle-aged, blond woman walked to the podium.

"Before I speak with you," Anne Marie said, "let me

ask you something. How many of you have people reporting to you, either at work or at home?" People laughed as most raised their hands. Anne Marie winked. "I bet a lot of you don't think of yourselves as being managers at home?" There was another murmur of pleased agreement.

"So you're all managing people in several parts of your life," Anne Marie continued. "Today I want to talk with you about motivating others. That's your job as leaders, you know. In the time we have together here, I will share with you a way to motivate people. It's the most powerful management truth I've ever found. It is simple. It is profound. And, as usual with simple and profound truths, it's right under your nose. When you leave here today, my guess is that you will start paying attention to your interactions with people in a whole new way—a way that will help you build positive relationships, increase people's energy, and improve their performance on the job. It may even make you better parents. It's all about what you focus on. What we need as managers and team leaders and parents is a way to focus on what is bright and noble and wonderful in the people we work with. Let me show you what I mean. Would everybody in the room please stand up?"

When the entire hall was on its feet, Anne Marie

said, "I have two tasks for you. First, for about a minute or so, I'd like you to greet people around you as if they're not important, and you're looking for someone else more important to talk to."

The auditorium was soon buzzing, as everyone exchanged cursory greetings and handshakes, mostly in low voices and without eye contact.

After a short while Anne Marie announced, "Okay, that's enough. Now, this time I'd like you to greet everybody around you, for another minute or so, as if they're long-lost friends and you're so glad to see them."

Instantly the place was alive with movement and loud voices. People were smiling warmly, shaking hands enthusiastically, and patting each other on the back.

This time when Anne Marie tried to intervene, it was more difficult. Even when she said, "You can sit down now," the noise level in the room remained high. People were having fun greeting each other this way.

Finally, when everyone was seated, Anne Marie asked, "Now, why did I have you do that?" Everyone laughed, as if they were wondering the same thing. "It was to make a point about energy," she continued. "I'm convinced that to motivate people and create a world-class organization or department, you have to know how to manage people's energy. Which of the two activities I asked you to engage in generated the most energy?"

"The second one!" the crowd answered.

"That's right. How did I increase the energy in the room? All I did was ask you to change what you focused your attention on. The first time you were focused on the negative—these were unimportant people, and you were looking for someone more important. The second time I gave you a positive focus—these were long-lost friends. Did that change in focus make a difference in your energy? It sure did!"

As Anne Marie Butler paused for a sip of water, the audience buzzed with enthusiasm, showing that her introduction had prepared them well. They were eager. They were ready. They were *motivated.*

"Now," Anne Marie continued, "how many of you have watched the Shamu killer whale show at one of the SeaWorld parks?" Again most of the hands in the room went up. "In getting to know Dave Yardley and his staff of animal trainers at the Orlando SeaWorld, I've been fascinated to learn the key to their phenomenal success in getting the whales to perform the feats they do.

"Now, you might be wondering, 'What in the world does the training of killer whales have to do with motivating my people at work or my kids at home?' The answer is—everything. The very methods they use to train these marvelous animals work just as well, if not better, with people. Why? Because we can *talk* to people. I want to share some of those methods with you this morning and have you think about applying them to the way you manage people. To begin with, I'm going to teach you what I call the ABC's of performance management." A slide appeared on the large screen behind the podium:

The ABC's of Performance

A = Activator

Whatever Gets Performance Going

B = Behavior

The Performance That Occurs

C = Consequence

Your Response to the Performance

"Let's start with the *A,* the Activator," Anne Marie said. "What we mean by an *Activator* is something that stimulates the behavior or performance that you want. The trainers at SeaWorld use signals to cue what they want the animals to do—arm or hand signals, slapping the water, or tooting a whistle. With people, an Activator can be a set of instructions, a training experience— or even a boss yelling at them. The most common Activators are goals. In my work with organizations I sometimes ask managers to tell me their people's goals. Then I go to the people and ask *them* what their goals are. When we put the two sets of goals together, they're almost always different. Often they don't even look similar. As a result, people are criticized by their bosses for not doing what they didn't know they were supposed to do in the first place. That's not a very effective way to manage or to be managed.

"All good performance starts with clear goals. If managers don't sit down with their people and develop smart, workable goals that are clear on both sides, their people are left without any idea of what they're expected to do or what good performance looks like. If your people don't know what they're being asked to do, what you do as a manager doesn't matter. Even Alice, in *Alice in Wonderland,* learned that. When she came to a fork in the road, she found the Cheshire Cat sitting there. She asked him, 'Which road should I take?' 'Where are you going?' asked the cat. 'I don't know,' said Alice. 'Then it doesn't matter,' the cat was quick to reply.

"So the *A* in the ABC—whatever triggers the performance—is important," Anne Marie continued, "but it certainly isn't the whole story. After you motivate the performance you want by setting clear goals, you have to observe the *behavior* that follows. That's what *B* stands for. With a killer whale, that behavior might be jumping into the air, giving a trainer a ride around the pool, splashing the audience with his tail, or taking a bow. With people at work, it might be talking effectively with customers, achieving a sales quota, or getting a report in on time. With kids, it might be cleaning their room or doing homework. Observing the behavior that occurs after initial activation is a step that is often missed by managers—even when they get the performance they want. Once goals are set and the necessary training is over, they disappear. When that happens, they don't have a prayer of taking advantage of the third and most important step in managing performance: the *C* or *Consequence*—what happens *after* you get the behavior you were looking for. But before we go on, let me ask you a very important question: When you do something right at work, what kind of response do you usually get?"

People stopped to think about that, then began to smile, and finally broke into laughter. Someone voiced what the audience was realizing by shouting out, "*Noth-ing* happens! Nobody says *any*thing!"

"You're absolutely right," Anne Marie agreed. "The most frequent response people get for their perfor-mance is *no* response. Nobody notices or comments until—when?"

Everyone in the audience knew what the answer to that question was: when things go wrong.

"When I ask people all around the world, 'How do you know when you're doing a good job?' the most common response I get is, 'When I haven't been chewed out lately by my boss.' In other words, no news is good news. But just take a look at this next slide . . ."

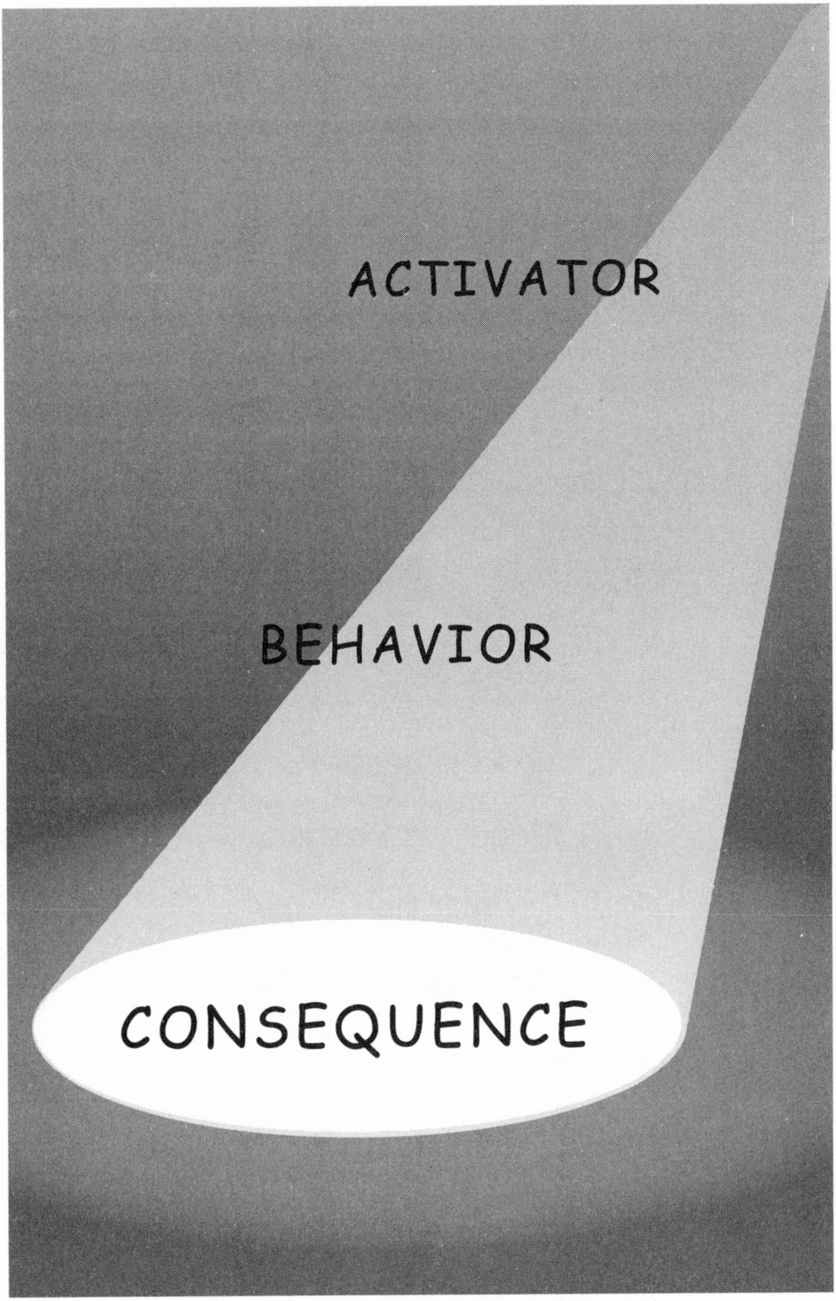
ACTIVATOR
BEHAVIOR
CONSEQUENCE

"Does everybody notice where the spotlight is?" Anne Marie asked. "That's to indicate that of the three steps, *A*, *B*, or *C*, *C* has by far the greatest impact on overall performance. Yet, as we all just recognized, the usual response we get to performing well is that we're left alone. Actually, there are three other kinds of responses you can make."

A new image appeared on the overhead screen:

4 Kinds of Consequences

1. No Response

2. Negative Response

3. Redirection

4. Positive Response

"To some degree, we've already covered the first two responses," Anne Marie said. "The most popular, of course, is the first, No Response. People are so accustomed to being ignored, they think of it as a normal condition of work. The response people really pay attention to is the Negative. Most people are managed by a *leave-alone-zap* approach. They never hear anything from their boss until they screw up. The No Response is followed by a Negative Response, which can come in the form of an angry look, verbal criticism, or even some kind of penalty.

"The last two responses on our list—Redirection and Positive—are the least used, yet they are the most powerful. Let's look at Redirection first. People say to me, 'You can't just ignore poor performance or negative behavior,' and I agree. What I learned from the whale trainers is that if these marvelous mammals do something unacceptable, the trainers *redirect* their energy and attention either back to what they were supposed to do or onto something else. Redirection is the most effective way to address undesirable behavior. Dave Yardley, my SeaWorld friend, told me that the trainers don't pay any attention to whales' poor behavior. Instead, they quickly redirect their attention to another task and then observe their performance closely so they can catch them doing something right.

"Now, how does Redirection work with people? First, let me tell you I think that Redirection is the best way to turn countless low-morale situations around. You will find this response will work in ninety-nine percent of the cases where you might be tempted to use a Negative Response on a person. It's a very powerful response because it gets the person back on track, and at the same time it maintains respect and trust by not calling attention to the off-course behavior in a negative way."

As Anne Marie continued talking, Wes Kingsley's eyes took on a faraway look as he remembered Mike Talmadge, his old boss at Benning Corporation, the best manager he'd ever had. From the moment Mike had hired him, Wes had felt the support of the older man. Mike's evident confidence in him made Wes want to succeed more than ever, and he had thrown himself into the job.

In his memory, Wes saw himself walking into Mike's office one day. Mike was sitting at his desk poring over some documents. When he looked up, his face was serious. "Sit down, Wes," he said. "We need to go over some things."

"Sure." Wes took a chair, puzzled by Mike's serious demeanor.

"These are reports of your sales for the past month," Mike began. "Some of them show that you've started calling on the people over at the Harrelson plant, right?" Wes nodded. "Did you know that Shauna Dietrich has had the Harrelson account for a year now?"

"My gosh, I had no idea!" Wes slapped his forehead in embarrassment.

"Okay." Mike sat back and smiled. "We've got to go over something. It's my fault. I obviously shortchanged you by not covering in detail how to keep track of what areas are being worked by whom." Mike turned his computer screen so Wes could see it. "Pull your chair up to the screen here. I can show you real quick how to access that information."

Wes felt a wave of relief. His boss's characteristic blaming of himself had taken the heat off. No longer apprehensive, Wes leaned forward eagerly as Mike explained his mistake.

Wes reviewed that meeting in detail. *First, Mike described my error without reproaching me. Second, he took the hit himself, removing the pressure I was feeling. That made me open and willing to learn. There was no hint of punishment. He went through the task I'd goofed up on in great detail, showing as well as telling me how it should be done. Finally, he expressed trust and confidence in me. When I left his office, I was completely back on track—and feeling even better about doing a good job for him and the company.*

Wes realized that he had just played out in his mind a perfect Redirection response. The proof, he concluded, was in the way he'd felt he had been treated by Mike, and in the renewal of his energy and commitment the session had produced. Only a few months after that, Wes had become the company's top salesperson and stayed there for the remainder of his time with Benning Corporation. As his attention returned to what Anne Marie was saying, a new slide appeared on the screen.

The Redirection Response

- Describe the error or problem as soon as possible, clearly and without blame.

- Show its negative impact.

- If appropriate, take the blame for not making the task clear.

- Go over the task in detail and make sure it is clearly understood.

- Express your continuing trust and confidence in the person.

Satisfied that he now understood the power of the Redirection response, Wes returned his full attention to the speaker. Anne Marie was saying, "The fourth reaction people can get to their performance is a Positive Response. The trainers at SeaWorld might give the whales a bucket of fish, rub their bellies, or give them toys or playtime. At work, the response might be giving praise or providing a learning opportunity, or even a promotion. With kids you praise them, reinforce with a hug, let them watch TV, or give them a treat or a special privilege. When a good performance is followed by something positive, naturally people want to continue that behavior. The intention of Redirection is to set up a Positive Response.

"It's important to emphasize here not to wait for *exactly right* behavior before you respond positively. Otherwise, you might wait forever."

Another new slide appeared on the screen:

Praise progress.
It's a moving target.

"This is exactly what the SeaWorld trainers do," Anne Marie continued. "If they want to teach a killer whale to jump out of the water and over a rope on a signal, how do you think they do that? Do you think they go out in the ocean with a boat and a megaphone and yell, 'Jump! Jump!' until some whale jumps over the rope extended over the side of the boat? That would be called 'hiring a winner.'

"When they first start training a new whale, he knows how to jump but he knows nothing about jumping over ropes. So they start with the rope underneath the water, high enough from the bottom for the whale to swim under it. If the whale swims under the rope, the trainers don't pay any attention. But every time he swims over the rope, they pay attention to him—they feed him.

"Now, Shamu is no idiot. After a while he says to himself, *Hm, there seems to be an interesting relationship going on here between this rope and food.* So he starts swimming over the rope more. Then what do you think the trainers do? They start raising the rope. Why do they do that? It's not a very exciting show if the trainer looks down in the water and says, 'Shamu did it again!' and the people are looking around, wondering where the whale is. They have to get him out of the water."

Wes chuckled with the rest of the audience.

"The point here is that progress—doing something better—is constantly being noticed, acknowledged, and rewarded. We need to do the same thing with people—catch them doing things better, if not exactly right, and praise progress. That way, you set them up for success and build from there."

Wes Kingsley had been listening carefully to Anne Marie's speech. Now, reminded by her remarks about praising progress, he had another flashback. This time he remembered the way he and his wife, Joy, as young parents, had taught their girls to walk. It had been such fun for them to stand one of them up and watch her delight as she swayed unsteadily—then plumped down on her little rear end with a charming chuckle. It was a game the three of them were playing, a loving game without rules.

But, he recognized now, *it was definitely a game with consequences.* Each time one of the little girls stood up, Mom and Dad would laugh and clap their hands. Cheered on by such an appreciative audience, what tyke would not repeat the performance?

Finally came the memorable moment when the youngster unexpectedly took a tentative step. Of course, she sat right down again, delighted with the burst of applause that greeted her achievement. Wes had grabbed her up and hugged her proudly. "You walked! You walked!" he repeated. Smiling now at the memory, Wes thought, *That was praising progress, all right. Good thing I didn't spank the kids when they didn't stand and walk perfectly the first time. We'd have had teenagers crawling around the house.*

"Now, let me ask you something," Anne Marie continued. "Which do you think is easier, catching people doing things wrong, or catching them doing things right?"

The group response was unanimous: "Wrong!"

"You've got *that* right! Great job!" she said, and her audience realized that she had just accentuated the positive with them in an exaggerated way.

"Catching people doing things wrong is easy," Anne Marie affirmed. "All you have to do is wait for them to foul up. Then you can look smart by pointing out their mistakes. I call that the GOTcha Response. Nothing to it. In fact, many bosses, as we've already suggested, are 'seagull' managers. They leave their people alone until they do something wrong. Then they swoop in, make a lot of noise, and dump on everybody. It's the old leave-alone-zap approach." Wes and many others in the audience could identify with that kind of treatment.

"Catching people doing things *right* is what I've come to call—if you'll pardon the pun—the WHALE DONE Response," Anne Marie said. The chuckles throughout the hall showed that people appreciated the pun. "That response is much harder because it takes patience and self-control. Especially if you've been ignoring what people do right and have been using lots of GOTchas, you must learn to observe what they are doing in a whole new way. You may even have to deliberately look past the undesirable behaviors that used to grab all your attention. In other words, you have to change what you are looking for. Your search for something done well may require greater effort, but it has far greater payoffs in generating the kind of behavior you want from your people at work and from your kids at home.

"It's good to keep positive responses flowing by inter-jecting little pats on the back like 'Nice going' and 'Good job.' I call these *attaboy* or *attagirl* responses. But the real WHALE DONE Response is more than that.

A genuine, full-blown WHALE DONE includes several steps . . ."

A new slide appeared:

The WHALE DONE Response

- Praise people immediately.

- Be specific about what they did right or almost right.

- Share your positive feelings about what they did.

- Encourage them to keep up the good work.

"I had an interesting experience several weeks ago that will illustrate the WHALE DONE Response," Anne Marie said. "I was visiting a regional manager of a retail chain who is a friend of mine. We walked into one of his stores, the store manager greeted us, and my friend said to her, 'Why don't you take us on a cheer-leading tour?' The manager looked blank until my friend said, 'Show us all the things that are going right around here.' The manager was delighted as she introduced her boss to her high-performing people and showed him the results of their good work. That gave her a chance to applaud her people right on the spot in front of her boss. It was obvious to me that that whole experience would encourage everyone to perform at a high level. 'But,' you might ask, 'wasn't the regional manager interested in the things that were not going so well?'

"Sure, but listen to what he told the store manager after the cheerleading tour: 'Now that I've seen everything that's going right, are there any problems you're facing that my staff and I at headquarters could help you with?' The manager, sensing that her boss meant her no harm, was now willing to talk about needed improvements."

Sitting in the audience, Wes Kingsley smiled as he remembered how Dave Yardley had told him how he had built trust with the whales using a no-harm approach.

"What I love about what that regional manager did," Anne Marie said, "is how he emphasized the positive first. He then permitted his manager to talk about things that were not going well—on *her* terms."

A new slide came up, reviewing the two responses Anne Marie had named:

GOTcha
Catching people doing things wrong

WHALE DONE!
Catching people doing things right

"If you grew up being GOTcha'd a lot, maybe you've tended to perpetuate it with others. But if your goal as a manager is performance improvement, it's vitally important you start using the WHALE DONE Response. I think you can begin to see that a lot of us often do things exactly backwards. We focus our attention on poor performance rather than on good performance. In the process, we reinforce the very behavior we don't want!

"Attention is like sunshine to humans. What we give our attention to, grows. What we ignore, withers. I'm going to point out a paradox that is responsible for most of the troubles we have in all our relationships, whether it's with the people who report to us at work, our spouses, or our kids at home. Think about this. When do you generally pay attention to people? It's when they're doing things wrong, isn't it? And when do you pay little attention to them? When everything's okay. For example, as parents we might say, 'The kids are playing well together. In fact, they're being fabulous. It's time for a little breather, right?' "

Anne Marie paused and looked around at her listeners. "*Wrong!* Right then, when things are going well, we lose a great motivational opportunity. We go brain-dead, become inactive, and don't pay attention or communicate. But if you were to systematically give people positive, specific feedback after they did something right, do you think you would get more of that behavior, or less of it?"

"More," the audience responded.

"Of course you would. That's why we need to wake up and do and say something positive and encouraging when people are exceeding expectations, or when they've corrected errors they've made. If I could light a fire under managers about one single thing, this would be it." Anne Marie turned and pointed at the overhead screen as it displayed a new slide:

Wake up and say something positive when everything is going well!

Wes Kingsley said to himself, *She's right, I need to start doing that more.*

"I want you to know," Anne Marie said, "that I realize switching your attention is not easy, particularly if you've gotten into the GOTcha habit—finding fault and criticizing others. You need a way to remind yourself to give people lots of WHALE DONEs. Just imagine, when you are with your people or your families, that every person is wearing a big sign that says, CATCH ME DOING SOMETHING RIGHT.

"I've seen WHALE DONE work so well in the business world that it turns teams and companies around. I encourage each one of you to start using this approach today, or tonight when you go home. Determine to respond positively to all the people around you. Once you start on this journey, and especially after you've had some early successes with it, you'll see how it will energize your relationships. Then you'll be encouraged to keep on with it.

"Sometimes, of course, you're going to forget and react negatively. You'll have a bad day, come home, and fly off the handle at someone. But if you make a conscious effort to emphasize the positive in all your relationships, eventually it will become a habit. And it's going to pay off in ways you can't imagine."

Wes wrote the phrase *Emphasize the positive in my relationships* in his notebook. Then he underlined it.

"I should mention," Anne Marie continued, "that WHALE DONE is likely to save you a lot of grief as well. I was standing in line at an airport ticket counter recently, and the guy ahead of me began giving the attendant all kinds of abuse. He complained about his reservations, shouted about the delay, and criticized the airline for inefficiency. He was openly sarcastic and rude. Finally as the attendant directed him to his gate and he walked away, it was my turn. I stepped up and said to her, 'That was great the way you handled that guy. I was amazed that you managed to stay so calm and composed!'"

" 'Thanks,' she said. 'I appreciate the compliment.

As for our happy friend, the fact is, he's going to Chicago but his bags are going to Seattle.' " When the laughter subsided, Anne Marie added, "Then she proceeded to upgrade me to first class.

"When you accentuate the positive, you'll begin to pay attention to what you do or say *after* people perform. I guarantee their performance will improve, and so will your relationships. Just remember, you're always reinforcing *some*thing—even when you're doing nothing. So, ask yourself about your responses. Are they No Responses? Are they Negatives? Are they Redirections, or are they Positives—WHALE DONEs? The more WHALE DONEs you do, the better.

"People ask me, 'What about unacceptable behaviors or poor performance on the job? How do you deal with those?' I usually recommend the Redirection response. But if somebody knows better and they continue with unacceptable behavior, that's an attitude problem. A Redirecting response will have little effect because they already know what to do. They need to know in no uncertain terms that what they are doing is unacceptable to you. But remember, a Negative response is a last resort. You tell people, immediately and specifically, what they did that was unacceptable—including the negative impact of their action and how you feel about it: disappointed, confused, frustrated. But since you don't want the focus to be on your feelings, always end that kind of message with an affirmation of the person. They need to know that it's the behavior, not them, that you find unacceptable.

"My feeling today," Anne Marie said, "is that things are changing so fast and frequently that few people ever get to be experts in their work. Most of us are constant learners, so if people make mistakes, Redirection is more appropriate than a Negative response, even if it ends with a reaffirmation.

"You should also remember that whenever you criticize someone's performance or give negative feedback, no matter how carefully you do it, it tends to harm or detract from your relationship with that person. If you keep it up, you will poison the relationship. They'll lose trust and start trying to get even with you. This is where it helps to think of a relationship as being like a bank account. If you give a Negative response to someone who knows better, it helps if you have money in that relationship bank—that is, if you've previously been giving that person lots of WHALE DONEs. Then he or she won't mind the correction. When the trust is there, a mistake can even lead to better performance. WHALE DONE—accentuating the positive—always creates a *con*structive cycle.

"Now, to let you know how much I appreciate the way you've been demonstrating the spirit of WHALE DONE with me here this morning, I have a gift for each of you." Anne Marie signaled to some people standing at the back of the auditorium with boxes in their hands. As they started down the aisles, passing objects out to the audience, she continued, "When you get your gift, you'll have what my friends at SeaWorld and I decided was the official symbol of WHALE DONE."

There was much commotion and excited comment in the crowd as people received and examined their gifts. Each was a beautifully shaped and realistically colored model of a leaping killer whale. On its belly was embossed the slogan WHALE DONE.

"You can use these gifts to start a movement in your organization," Anne Marie explained. "If you catch somebody doing something right, give that person a killer whale and ask him to pass it on to someone else who's doing something right. If you need more whales, let me know. I guarantee they will literally work like a charm."

Anne Marie's mixture of inspiration and practical advice had obviously hit home with the audience. When she ended her speech, they acknowledged her with a standing ovation. As the applause slackened,

loudspeakers started to play a song that sounded familiar to Wes. Many people in the smiling crowd began to
sing along.

You got to ac-cen-tuate the positive, e-lim-inate the negative,
Latch on to the affirmative. . . .

Chapter Three

"IS THAT YOU, WES? HOW ARE YOU?"

Wes rose from his seat at the table in the coffee shop where he'd been waiting for Anne Marie. "I enjoyed your talk," he said. "Thanks for inviting me!"

They sat down and ordered coffee. "So, you got to spend time with my friend Dave Yardley at SeaWorld," Anne Marie said. "Did you meet his teacher?"

"You mean Shamu. Dave and his teacher were very good to me. How did you come to know Dave?"

Anne Marie smiled and settled back in her seat. Wes decided she rarely missed an opportunity to tell a story.

"One day," she began, "when I was working with a large corporate client in Florida, I brought one of my classes out to SeaWorld, and we saw the Shamu show. Did you see it?"

"I did." Wes replied.

"Isn't it wonderful? Those whales are magnificent.

They got me thinking. Whenever I walk into a store or a restaurant or a place of business and see life and passion and sparkle in the place, I want to know why. What created that great environment where people are genuinely excited about the work they do? When I went to the Shamu show and saw how the trainers and the whales seemed to be having such a good time, and how powerfully that enjoyment was transferred to the audience, I wanted to find out their management secrets. So, just as you did, I approached the trainer— our friend Dave Yardley—and asked him about it. Lo and behold, the training principles they were using with the whales turned out to be the same ones I was teaching to managers! That's when I started to call catching people doing things right the WHALE DONE approach."

"Your talk certainly squared with what I learned during my own day at SeaWorld," Wes said. "Dave told me that the basis of everything they do with the animals is the principle of *no harm*—creating trusting, positive relationships with them. Obviously, No Response or a Negative Response can be detrimental to what they're trying to get the whales to do. On the other hand, Positive Responses—and particularly your WHALE DONE Response—would be essential. But the concept I really am fascinated with is the Redirection Response. That's the one people are going to ask about, because of their concerns about how to handle inappropriate behavior or unacceptable performance."

"You're right," Anne Marie said. "The Redirecting Response is very important."

"As I understand it," Wes said, "handled properly, it can lead to a WHALE DONE if you catch people correcting their mistakes or improving their performance. That leads to a more trusting relationship."

"You're absolutely right, Wes. A lot of people don't make that connection."

"I guess I'm interested in all this because it's kind of counter to my background—I mean what's been handed down from my father and the teachers and bosses I've had over the years."

"Lots of 'my way or the highway' stuff, huh?"

"Exactly," Wes said. "I've never lacked for role models in being a GOTcha manager and parent."

"That's a very common thing. It's the ripple effect of GOTcha. The boss yells at one of his managers, that manager yells at one of his associates, who goes home and yells at his spouse, who yells at the kid, who kicks the cat."

"You know, Anne Marie," Wes said reflectively, "it's

really strange. All this emphasis on the positive seems to be boring new channels in my gray matter. Both times—when I was at SeaWorld with Dave, and listening to you today—I've started to imagine interacting differently with the people in my life. I've thought, 'Why *not* start accentuating the positive? Those folks have been doing things right all around me for a long time, and I've simply taken it for granted. They deserve better.' Now that's radical thinking for me. I guess as soon as people do a task correctly, I should give them a WHALE DONE, right?"

"Not exactly."

Wes looked puzzled.

"I'm only objecting to your word 'correctly,' " Anne Marie said. "It sounds like you're going to wait until they do it *perfectly* right. Remember what I said about how the SeaWorld people train the whales to jump out of the water?"

"They reward progress—any movement in the desired direction."

"Exactly! Follow the same rule."

"That makes sense," Wes said. "But aren't you sometimes asked if the WHALE DONE Response isn't manipulation? I understand why the whales get a reward when they do something the trainer wants them to do, but I guess I object to the concept of human behavior being managed solely by rewards and recognition. People aren't whales. They have minds of their own and don't do things others want or need done just because they expect to be rewarded. They do them because they think they're the right things to do."

Anne Marie nodded in agreement. "I'm very glad you brought that up. There are two points about manipulation. First of all, the only people who don't need to be motivated by others are entrepreneurs—people who either own their own businesses or are individual contributors working for themselves. They are self-motivated and their goals are aligned with the organizational goals. In fact, their personal goals and organizational goals are usually the same. Everyone else—employees, children at home, or the whales at SeaWorld—is asked to do things the organization needs them to do, but which they might not choose to do on their own."

"Like my kids having to keep their rooms clean at home," Wes said with a grin.

"Exactly," said Anne Marie. "So, finding out what motivates people is important. Secondly, you don't want people to become dependent solely on your noticing and commenting, so they do well only when you're around. The point of good management is to influence people to do the right thing when you're *not* around. No manager wants his people to perform well just because they're looking for praises or raises. Nor do we want our kids to look for a cookie every time they behave well or perform a household chore. Instead of building dependency on others for a reward, you want people to do the right thing because they themselves enjoy it. Like those killer whales you saw in the Shamu show, having such fun performing for the crowd. The ultimate goal of the WHALE DONE Response is to help people become self-motivating."

"You mean, so that the WHALE DONEs are coming from inside themselves?"

"Right. You want people to start catching *themselves* doing things right, and act accordingly."

"How do you do that?"

"There are various ways. After giving lots of WHALE DONEs, you start to make comments like 'I'll bet it felt good when you finished that project before the deadline' or 'You must be proud of what you did on that report.' Or, when you know that they must be feeling good about their performance, you can say, 'Tell me how that feels,' or, 'What's it like, to have done such a good job?' Then really listen to them and reinforce their pride and feeling of accomplishment."

"I get it," said Wes, nodding in understanding. "So even the WHALE DONE Response is not an end in itself. It's a lead-up to the ultimate goal of helping people catch themselves doing things right."

"Bingo!"

"That's great. By the way, Anne Marie, who taught you to accentuate the positive?"

"My father," she answered. "He was a career navy man and he told me early in life, 'It's great to have a position of power, but don't use it. The only way you can really get people to do what you want them to do is by developing a positive, trusting relationship with them. Be positive with people and you'll get positive results.' " She looked at her watch. "I've got to catch a cab to the airport. I'm giving a speech in Chicago tomorrow and promised to have dinner tonight with the conference organizers."

"Let me drive you," insisted Wes, seizing the opportunity to spend more time with his new mentor.

Wes paid the check and they left the coffee shop, walking through the lobby to the hotel entrance where they waited briefly for Wes's car. Once they were on the way to the airport, Anne Marie said, "I can see you're determined to get back home and start catching people doing things right. But I'd also like you to think of using the WHALE DONE Response as a strategy for your company. Organizations whose managers are serious about this concept and have put it in place are finding out that it directly affects their bottom line."

"How so?" Wes asked.

"Any new business improvement today, whether it's a technology or a service innovation or a pricing strategy, becomes instantly known and copied by the competition. That means that your only real competitive edge is your relationship with your people. If they trust and respect you and believe in your goals, they will want to please your customers. When that happens, provided you've got other factors like product quality, pricing and marketing, and delivery in place, no one can beat you. *The one thing your competition can never steal from you is the relationship you have with your people, and the relationship they have with your customers.*"

"In your talk this morning," Wes said, "I was struck by your point that we are *always* reinforcing something by our response to others' behavior. I never realized that I have an impact on people's performance even when I'm ignoring them. Now that I recognize the power of WHALE DONE, I'm planning to make it my very first priority in building trusting relationships and motivating my people."

"Remember, though," Anne Marie warned, "that

individuals are motivated by different things. The SeaWorld trainers learned that, except for food, what works with one animal may not work with another. That made them start observing the whales closely to find out what each of them liked or didn't like. A WHALE DONE Response is a good start, but after a while it may ring hollow. Knowing the particular things that motivate and compel each person helps you add power to their motivation."

"And is observing people the best way to find out what motivates them?" Wes said.

"It's one way. As I mentioned, one of the great advantages we have with people is that we can talk to them."

"In other words, I should *ask* my people what motivates them?"

"Yes. Say to them, 'I know you have been doing a good job on that inventory problem. What's the best way I could recognize your efforts, in the short run and the long run?"

"What do you mean by short run *and* long run?" Wes asked.

"Short run has to do with what would motivate that person on a day-to-day basis. Long run has to do with appropriate recognition for a particular performance

period—monthly, quarterly, yearly, etc. But the important thing to remember, whether you're talking short or
long run, is not to *assume* you know what is motivating
that person."

"Can you give me an example?"

"Sure. Suppose you're pleased with someone's
performance and say, 'In recognition of the great job
you've been doing with customer relations, I'm giving
you more responsibility.' However, in this case the
person has had some health problems in the family and
could use some extra cash.

"Then you might tell someone else who is due for a
big WHALE DONE, 'I'm so pleased with your work,
I've negotiated a nice raise for you.' But in this case the
person doesn't have pressing financial needs and might
be saying to herself, 'What I'd really like instead is to
have more responsibility around here.' So what have
you done? You've given a raise to someone who'd like
more responsibility, and more responsibility to someone who needs a raise."

"So the rule," Wes said, "is . . ."

Never assume you know what motivates a person.

"That's why it never hurts to ask," Anne Marie said.

As they drove onto the freeway, the two sat quietly for a few moments. Then Wes broke the silence. "Correct me if I'm wrong, but you shouldn't come up with a WHALE DONE response mechanically. If you're just going through the motions—'Oh, nice job, Herb, keep up the good work,' and so on—people will know you don't really mean it."

"I agree. Dave learned that from the killer whales. He discovered that if you're insincere with a whale, the animal will know. You can't fool killer whales. They feel the insincerity in your hands when you give them a rubdown. When the animal knows you're not interested, he won't want to work with you. He'll swim away."

"Around my company," Wes said, "insincerity is sometimes called blowing smoke or polishing the apple. People can see right through phony praise. It makes them suspicious and they'll 'swim away' in a hurry."

"Many managers breed mediocrity that way," Anne Marie said. "The only time they pay attention to what somebody does is when that person is *not* performing at a certain level. So when managers suddenly use praise or encouragement or rewards, it doesn't ring true. The person thinks, 'What is my boss up to now?' It comes across as manipulation."

Wes frowned. "Frankly, that's got me worried. I have such a GOTcha history with my people. What happens if I jump the tracks and start accentuating the positive, or changing my negative feedback into redirecting? Won't they see right through it?"

Anne Marie nodded. "My rule about that is . . ."

WHALE DONE only works when you're sincere and honest.

"If you suspect that your people think your positive responses are insincere," Anne Marie said, "take the time to prove otherwise. Anticipate your team's reaction and be honest with them. Admit you've been too negative and that you want to change that. Share the

WHALE DONE method with them, and ask for their help."

They had reached the terminal and were turning up the Departing Flights ramp when Anne Marie offered her final piece of advice. "We've got plenty of data on the failure of GOTcha to produce the results we want, both in terms of productivity and human satisfaction. What I'd like to see is large numbers of business managers using the WHALE DONE Response in a deliberate, systematic way. Don't be afraid to involve your people. And remember, catch *yourself* doing things right. Praise your own progress. And be patient. When something is worth doing, keep doing it."

"Wish me luck," Wes said as they pulled up in front of the terminal entrance.

"You'll do fine." Anne Marie shook Wes's hand warmly. Reaching into her travel case, she handed Wes some printed sheets of paper. "We were talking about sincerity, and how important it is in dealing with people. But sometimes it's hard to know what to say. Here are some examples that might help you get started." She handed Wes her business card. "Stay in touch. Keep me posted on how it's going."

Wes had the distinct impression that she meant it, that her support of him would be active and ongoing. He looked at the sheets she had given him.

Some "Whale Done" Responses

At Work

To a manager:

• When you contributed your piece in the meeting, it was a standout. Your opening was designed to draw attention, and I saw Ms. A's face light up when you made your points about X and Y. What you did in that short time has really helped to ensure the confidence of that client. It made us all look good! Thanks. Keep up the good work.

To a work team:

• This team is going off the charts in terms of working together smoothly and assuming responsibility. In taking over the leadership, you all have helped me move to the role of a coordinator, rather than a boss. I like that much better. Let's continue to work well as a team.

To an individual contributor:

• I liked the way you created these categories for the figures in your report. It makes it much easier to read the results. I'm going to recommend that we all use your system from now on. I'll look to you in the future for more good ideas.

~~~~

At Home

To a teenage son:
_____

- It really made me feel good when I came home and found you'd cleaned up the garage. I thought I was going to have to take this Saturday to do it, but now that it's done, I can relax and do other things. That's a real load off my mind, Bud. I sure do thank you.

To a first-grader:
_____

- You've been getting up the first time I've called you in the morning. Do you know how much that helps me, when we're all running around getting ready to go our separate ways? A lot!

To a twelve-year-old daughter:
_____

- I enjoy the conversations we've been having as we drive to your sports and lessons. It's fun to hear what's happening with you and your friends. Thanks. I hope we can continue this as you get older.

To a preschooler:
_____

- You tied your own shoes and picked out your clothes without any help. That's wonderful! Keep up the good work. I'm proud of you.

Some Redirection Responses

At Work

- Bill, I know you're having trouble with our new accounting system, so I'm asking Betty to give you a hand. (Later) Nice going, Bill. The report you turned in shows you're getting on top of the new system. Let me know if you have any questions.

- We want to make sure everyone's talents are used to the max on this project, Alison. That's why I'm assigning you to Team George; they can utilize all your skills over there. (Later) Congratulations, Alison. I knew you were the right person to work with Team George. I'm getting rave notices on your work.

At Home

[The youngster has not been doing a good job feeding the animals.]

- I'm switching your chores from feeding the pets to doing the vacuuming. I know you like to do that and we need it done. (Later) The house looks so nice since you took over the vacuuming!

[The kids are squabbling over the TV.]

- We need to develop a plan for watching TV so everybody is happy. (Later) I'm so proud of the way you two have been following the TV-watching plan you worked out when we sat down in the kitchen the other day.

Wes Kingsley tucked Anne Marie's lists into his briefcase, along with his notes from her lecture. It may have been a coincidence that he had met Dave Yardley and Anne Marie Butler. But it was no coincidence that he was beginning to feel a lot more self-confident about his abilities as a manager.

Chapter Four

THE FIRST DAY BACK AT WORK after meeting with Anne Marie Butler, Wes had an unexpected opportunity to use a WHALE DONE Response. He had spent the morning gathering information about anything positive that had happened since his Florida trip. In the afternoon he put it to use with Merideth Smalley, the leader of one of his accounting teams.

Wes and Merideth had been avoiding each other for nearly a year, ever since she thought that Wes had implied in a meeting that her group was responsible for a missed deadline. Their strained relationship had worsened when Wes, who played on the softball team that Merideth captained at the company picnic, had hit into a double play to lose an important game. Neither incident had sat well with Merideth, who was a sports enthusiast and very competitive.

Walking down the hallway, Wes spotted Merideth

coming toward him. She saw him and began to hurry by, but Wes stopped her. "Excuse me, Merideth. I need a moment of your time."

Glancing at her watch, Merideth murmured, "A moment is about what I've got."

Wes deliberately didn't hurry. His voice was relaxed and friendly as he said, "I'm very impressed by the way you have been dealing with our suppliers."

"Really?" Still avoiding his eyes, Merideth showed by her tone that she was suspicious.

"I've hassled with some of those people about late orders," Wes said, "and frankly I haven't had much success. But somehow you get it done. Case in point: I just got an order from Lukas Packing—the first one we've received on time from them, ever! I was so blown away I called the guy to tell him I appreciated it. Guess who he gave the credit to?"

Merideth's face broke into a smile she couldn't hide. She was plainly not used to receiving compliments, but there was no denying Wes's facts, or his sincerity. "Did you speak to John?" she asked excitedly. "He's the fierce one. I just talk turkey to him. I say, 'Listen. We have dealers who get supplies to us on time consistently, and we show our appreciation by giving them more busi-ness. Now, how about you?' The guy didn't know what to say . . ." Merideth was suddenly acting as if she had all day to talk.

"Let me run this by you," Wes interrupted. "June and Edmundo have also been struggling with this supplier. They need coaching. Would you be willing to work with them? They could learn a lot from you."

"Of course," Merideth said brightly. "No problem."

Back in his office, Wes sat down and analyzed the interaction with Merideth. What had really happened in those few minutes? he wondered. It all went so fast, he didn't want to assume too much. There definitely had been a change in Merideth's attitude and her willingness to cooperate with his request. Was she sincere? He felt as if a weight was lifting from his shoulders, but he didn't know how to deal with it. It all seemed too easy. *Okay,* he thought, *that went pretty well. But I've got my doubts about the meeting tomorrow.*

Wes had called a meeting of his six top managers for the next morning. He planned to get some business items and announcements out of the way first. But when he thought of what was next on the agenda, he felt uncomfortable.

When it was time for the meeting that morning, Wes lingered in his office. Again and again he had reviewed the notes he had taken from his SeaWorld trip and Anne Marie Butler's speech. How would his managers react to his sharing what he had learned? He particularly recalled what Anne Marie had said to him on the way to the airport: "Anticipate your team's reaction and be honest with them. Admit you've been too negative and that you want to change that. Share the WHALE DONE method with them, and ask for their help."

Here's hoping it works, Wes thought to himself as he closed his notebook. *If it does, I owe it all to you, Shamu.*

As usual Wes's managers stopped talking when he entered the room and sat down. This formality, the general distancing of his staff, was something Wes regretted. It had been like that ever since he was promoted over Harvey Meehan. As usual, Harvey's eyes were avoiding his. He started the meeting and soon all the preliminary items were out of the way. Wes paused and looked around the room. Then he cleared his throat and began to speak.

"I've got something to say to you that's hard for me. I've been making things rough for you people around here. I've been jumping all over you when you make even the smallest mistake, and completely ignoring you when you're doing an excellent job. I just haven't shown any appreciation for your efforts. That's going to change. Something happened to me on my recent trip that I hope will make a difference in the way I respond to your work." Then Wes began to tell the group about his trip to SeaWorld, his meeting with Dave Yardley, and his time with Anne Marie Butler. As he talked, he was aware that people were listening intently. Things seemed to be going well until, halfway through his talk, he saw Harvey Meehan look over at his pal Gus Sulermo and roll his eyes. The meaning was not lost on Wes. Harvey had been resistant to him ever since the promotion.

Despite knowing that Harvey's nonverbal put-down had been visible to the others, Wes went on. "I've come to understand what a positive difference it makes in their motivation when people are appreciated for what they do right." After explaining the difference between a WHALE DONE Response and a GOTcha Response, he confessed, "I think you'll all agree that I've been a pretty straight GOTcha kind of manager. I want to start being a WHALE DONE manager. The trouble is, that calls for a complete reversal of my behavior patterns with all of you. I'm aware enough to know that without some assistance I may just fail miserably at breaking my old habits. So I'm asking for your help."

There was a long pause. People around the table looked at each other uncertainly.

"I'll give you some help right now," a voice said. It was Merideth. Considering her past history with Wes, everyone expected her to speak out in criticism. Wes steeled himself for the worst.

"As most of you know," Merideth began, "Mr. Kingsley and I have not been the best of buddies. Given a choice, I've tried to avoid him. But yesterday he stopped me in the hall and insisted on talking with me. I was hesitant at first, expecting that he'd found something to climb on my case about. Instead, I found Wes was going out of his way to compliment me about my work. I knew he was sincere because he'd done his homework and mentioned some positive feedback he had from one of our suppliers. It made me feel good."

Turning to Wes, Merideth continued, "We all bust our humps around here, and we don't do it just for recognition. But I have to admit that being noticed does mean a lot. The recognition you gave me yesterday started to change my attitude toward you—and my work. Now that I see you reaching out to all of us, I want to be of any help I can."

Wes glanced around the room. Harvey continued to

roll his eyes cynically to Gus, and Wes could tell that most others in the group had yet to be convinced. "Thanks, Merideth," he said. "I do have a way that all of you can help me make this change. I want each of you to tell me how I can recognize and respond to your good performance in a way that will be most meaningful and rewarding for you."

After an uncomfortable moment of silence, Chuck Wilkins said, "I'll take a shot. When my mom was dying of cancer, the people at Hospice Center were so fabulous to us, and I've thought about doing some volunteer work there. My kids are active in sports, so my weekends are full. If I could spend an hour or two on occasional weekdays at the Hospice Center, when my work is caught up . . ."

"I think we can work that out, Chuck," Wes said. "Thanks."

Two others volunteered ideas, but everyone else sat stolidly, and as the meeting drew to a close, Wes was aware that not everyone was taking him seriously. "No doubt some of you are taking all this talk of mine with a grain of salt," he said. "Knowing my record, I don't blame you. You doubters can be my coaches. Whenever you catch me reverting to my old GOTcha game of accentuating the negative, I want you to speak up and call me on it."

Everyone filed out of the room without stopping to talk, but Wes knew there would be plenty of discussion around the watercooler and out in the parking lot. When he got back to his office, he found Anne Marie Butler's card and called her number. Incredibly, she came on the line. "Anne Marie? Hi. So good to hear your voice! It's Wes Kingsley. How are you?"

Anne Marie's high energy came rocketing through the receiver. "Wes! How good of you to call. What's been happening?"

Wes told her about his experience with Merideth and what he had said at the meeting. "Everyone seemed to be listening, but I think most of them have a wait-and-see attitude."

"That's okay, Wes," Anne Marie said reassuringly. "You made a good start."

"Thanks. I'm still feeling a little skeptical myself, and encouragement from you helps a lot. By the way, I want to order a box of those little toy whales you gave out during your speech. I'd like to use them with my people at work and my kids at home."

He gave Anne Marie his address and she said, "Okay, Wes, you're off and running. Be sure to call me every now and then to let me know your progress. And have lots of fun catching people doing things right."

When Wes had first returned from his Florida trip, he had tried to share with his wife, Joy, what he'd learned from Dave Yardley and Anne Marie Butler. But she was clearly not ready to hear it. Recently there had been a lot of tension in their relationship, and Wes realized that for some time now Joy had been emphasizing the negative, actively catching him doing things wrong. Whenever he got home late, she would unload on him. It wasn't a lot of fun. So rather than push his newfound knowledge on her, Wes had decided to use the WHALE DONE first at the office.

But one night when he got home from work, he found an unexpected opportunity to broach the subject again. Wes entered the house to hear Joy arguing with Allie, their fourteen-year-old. "I'm sick of this!" Joy was shouting. "Every day lately I come home exhausted from work and this kitchen is a pigsty. You and your friends never put anything away after you have your snacks. If I have to tidy up this place before I can make dinner one more evening, young lady, you're going to find yourself going hungry!"

Allie fled upstairs with a wounded look. And when Joy saw Wes, she was so angry with Allie that she didn't turn on him. In fact, she came toward him and started to cry. Wes took her in his arms and held her until she had calmed down. Then he said, "I know it's been pretty rough around here lately. Allie's been giving me a hard time, too. The girls are fighting a lot, and you and I always seem to be getting on each other's nerves. I think it's time for us to take a long weekend and go to Florida."

"Florida! What's there?"

"Killer whales," Wes said with a smile.

A couple of weekends later, Wes and his family found themselves flying south to Orlando. Ever since her blowup with her mother, Allie's mood at home had been dark. Now, while her younger sister, Meg, played and chattered away in the seat next to her, Allie sat gazing out the window in a funk. Finally she said, "This vacation sucks. Mom probably won't let me go anywhere or do anything fun."

Meg tried to cheer her up. "Daddy says the whale show is neat!"

"Big deal," Allie muttered, rolling her eyes. "I've seen aquariums before. This whole trip is *so* lame!"

Notwithstanding Allie's negative attitude, the family

was ecstatic when they saw the SeaWorld whales perform. Before the show began, Allie had sat long-faced and slumped over, but her entire posture changed as the giant whales went through their paces. At the end of the performance, she admitted it had been "wicked cool."

After leaving the stadium, Wes took Joy and the girls backstage, using the special pass Dave Yardley had left for them at the gate. When Wes and Dave saw each other, they shook hands warmly, and following introductions, Dave led them over to a training pool. An attractive young trainer in a black wet suit was kneeling at the pool's edge and rubbing the back of one of the whales.

"This is Pam Driscoll," Dave said. Pam gave a hand signal, and the huge animal turned over slowly and she began rubbing his white belly.

"Wow!" exclaimed Allie. "I do that with our dog at home. Is he a pet of yours?"

"Not exactly," Pam answered. "He's my friend. We love to pal around with each other."

"How do you get him to do what you want?" Joy asked. "Somehow I don't think he'd be intimidated by threats or punishments."

"You're right," Dave said. "Killer whales can 'take out' any other animal in the ocean. We sometimes use that information when we're working with dog trainers. Some of them scold and yell at their animals. They use choke chains and sometimes hit them. When they talk about that kind of treatment, I ask them, 'If your dog weighed eleven thousand pounds like Shamu, the whale, how would you treat him? Would you use a choke collar or smack him around? I don't *think* so."

"No way," Allie agreed.

"If you don't develop a friendly relationship with these whales and display a negative attitude toward them," Dave said, "they'll let you know right away that they don't like it."

"How do you avoid that reaction?" Joy asked.

"Rather than focusing on the negative—what they do wrong—we pay attention to what they do right," Dave answered. "We always try to catch the whales doing things right."

Seeing an opportunity, Allie put in, "I wish my mom and dad would catch Meg and me doing things right, instead of always getting on our case!"

Embarrassed by his daughter's remark, Wes started to reply sharply, then held his tongue. Turning to Dave, he said, "I was wondering if you'd have time to share some more of your training techniques with Joy and me."

Dave readily agreed. Realizing that Meg and Allie wanted to see more of SeaWorld, Pam volunteered to show them around.

On the way back to the office Wes told Dave about his meeting with Anne Marie Butler and some of the changes he was trying to make in his relationships at work. Then he said, "This trip I'm hoping Joy and I can come away with some ideas from the whales that will help us to improve our relationships with our kids. Now that Allie's a teenager, we can use all the help we can get."

They entered a training room off the office. "This is where we hold seminars and briefing sessions for our staff and visitors," Dave explained.

As they took comfortable chairs, Joy said, "I don't mean to change the subject, Dave, but when Wes says *we*, he's really not including himself too seriously in the parenting dilemma."

"Why is that?"

"Because he's never home. We both work, but he often stays late at the office. I teach part-time, so I'm usually there by the time the kids get home. Ninety-nine percent of the child-rearing responsibility falls on me. I'm the one who has to deal with the housekeeping details, the girls' homework, and refereeing their squabbles."

Wes was embarrassed. He couldn't believe that Joy was bringing this up in front of Dave.

Sensing Wes's discomfort, Dave said, "I don't want to get involved in a domestic scene, Joy, but it sounds to me as if you don't think Wes is home enough."

"You've got *that* right!"

"Mind if I ask you something? What do you do when he finally does come home?"

"What do you mean?"

"By any chance, do you take that opportunity to hassle him for not getting home earlier?"

"You've got that right, too!" Wes blurted out in his own defense.

"Okay," Dave said. "Let's pursue this problem from the standpoint of a killer whale trainer. We've already found that praise works better than blame in getting the animals to do what we want."

Joy looked indignant. "Are you suggesting that I praise Wes and make a fuss over him when he finally does come home?"

"Our success with the whales happens a little bit at a time," Dave explained. "We can't wait until they behave exactly as we want before we praise them."

"Always praise progress. It's a moving target," Wes

chimed in, remembering a phrase from his notebook. Then he said to Joy, "I'm sorry to have to say this, but whenever I leave work, it's like going from the frying pan into the fire. If you did as Dave has suggested, I'd be motivated to find ways to leave work early and come home earlier."

"Really." Joy's tone was thoughtful.

"Don't be discouraged, Joy," Dave said. "It seems GOTcha comes more easily to most of us than WHALE DONE."

Meanwhile, Pam had been showing Allie and Meg the animals and talking with them about the WHALE DONE method of training them. After they had visited the dolphins leaping and playing in their pools and were headed back to join their parents, Pam said, "So, what have you girls learned today?"

"Always be nice to the animals," Meg said, "especially when they're being good."

"Great. And what about when they don't behave so well?"

"I know you said we should ignore that behavior," Allie said, obviously puzzled.

"Right," said Pam. "If you pay attention when they're naughty, they'll keep on misbehaving because they like the attention."

"But that's so hard!" Allie said. "Suppose Meg comes into my room and starts messing with my computer stuff. Do I just look the other way?"

Pam smiled. "No, you can't really do that. But it doesn't make sense to just get mad. You two would need to sit down and work out some rules about using the computer. Is it all right with you if Meg uses it?"

"Yeah," Allie answered reluctantly. "But only if I'm not around. And never when I've got an important project."

"Okay, so you work things out in a way that Meg gets to use the computer some of the time, but never when it interferes with your needs. Now, I'm going to let you girls in on a secret formula we use when we train Shamu and the other whales. We focus on what they do *right* and reward them for that. For example, Allie, you could wait until you see that Meg is following the rules, then catch her doing things right and give her a WHALE DONE. You can tell her, 'I feel good about the way you've been following our rules, so I'm going to do the dishes for you tonight to show you I appreciate it.'"

"I know that's being nice and all, but how will that help?" Allie asked, frowning.

"Oh! Can I tell?" Meg asked, raising her hand as if she were in a classroom. "It's so I'll want to *keep on* following the rules."

"It might work, at that," Allie concluded.

"I'm going to focus on the positive, too," Meg chimed in. "My friend Sissie Lawrence has been real stuck-up lately. Now I think I know how to get her to play with me."

"How?" Pam asked with genuine interest.

"I'll watch her, and when she does something nice, I'll smile and thank her. I'll catch her doing something right."

Allie put her arm around her sister. "Meg can be real smart sometimes," she said proudly.

Back in the training room with Wes and Dave, Joy hadn't anticipated learning information from a whale trainer that could improve her relationship with her husband, especially when it called for a change in *her* behavior to bring about the desired change in *his*. She felt resistant to the idea that she should have to change

first. On the other hand, she was smart enough to realize that she was getting an important message. "So,"
she said, "the key to having a good relationship,
whether it be with your whales, my husband and our
kids, is to accentuate the positive."

"Absolutely," Dave replied. "It's not just about being
nice. It's about getting results. Here at SeaWorld we accentuate the positive because we realize the payoffs.
Not only does focusing on the positive motivate the behavior we want, it builds the trust and the fun-loving
kind of environment we need to work successfully with
these animals. People who see the show tell us they can
actually feel that positive energy operating here. They
can hardly believe that the whales are so responsive.
What's funny is that they also frequently comment
about how cooperative and energetic our staff is, but
they often don't put the two together. They act as if it's
an accident that morale here is so high. They don't see
that staff members are behaving with each other ac-
cording to the same principles we use with the animals.

"Rewards aren't the issue. Trust is the issue. Fun is
the issue. If we're not having fun—if the whales aren't
having fun, if our people aren't having fun—then
forget it."

"As we were preparing to make this trip," Joy said,
"Wes told me a little bit about WHALE DONE and

the importance of what you do *after* people do something. He also told me you ignore poor behavior and redirect the whales' energy onto something else that can set up a positive response. I have a little problem with that. I can understand how it might work with animals, but isn't it kind of hard to do with people?"

"You're right." Dave smiled. "It *is* hard—not so much because people are so difficult, but because through practice we've trained our attention to notice only what they do wrong. We have our eye out for the negative behavior. We think it deserves much more attention. That's why we jump all over it and make a big deal out of it. Plus, those people that get labeled as difficult always have people around them looking for them to goof up again. It's a self-fulfilling prophecy."

"I know I do a lot of that with Allie lately," Joy mused. "Especially when I'm tired."

"When you're tired, you probably ought to practice redirecting. In fact, when you're first starting out, you'll actually find yourself redirecting a lot—in place of the negative responses you've been giving. In many cases, your first positive responses will follow right after redirecting. You observe their new efforts, and see how quickly you can accentuate the positive and catch them making progress in the new direction.

"After a while, the person finds out you're basically

treating him much more decently and fairly, while still requiring high standards. See, in actual practice, 'ignoring' behavior means just not giving what people do wrong all the scrutiny and energy we usually give it. We say ignore it, because people usually seem to throw big searchlights on a misdirected action—sort of like on an escaping prisoner going over the wall! Our usual rule in working with the whales is to ignore them when they don't do it right, but stick around and redirect their actions. Then as soon as they make a right move, hit them with a WHALE DONE!"

"That's just the opposite of what people tend to do, isn't it?" Joy said. "I see why this technique requires attention. Timing is so important. If you're going to reward good behavior, you really have to be awake, especially with kids. You don't have any spare ideas around about how to use this technique as a mom, do you?"

"Not as a mom, but as a dad," Dave answered. "I'd been working with Shamu and the other killer whales for several years before my twins arrived. When Nat and Reid came along, my wife, Helene, and I wanted to see how WHALE DONE would work with the kids. At first we watched other parents to see what they were doing. Typically they'd relax when things were going well. With a baby, that meant not crying. With youngsters it meant behaving properly. With teens it meant not getting into trouble. It wasn't until the baby cried, the youngsters began to fight, or the teens brought home bad grades that parenting kicked in.

"Helene and I decided to be more proactive about our parenting. When our twin boys were babies, we played with them when they were happy. When they cried and we were sure they weren't wet, hungry, or sick, we didn't pay that much attention to them. But the moment they calmed down, we'd pick them up and cuddle them. When they grew older we started observing them closely. You can always tell, if you're observant, when kids are getting bored or restless. That's when they start to fight or get into trouble. If you're on your game, you'll change or redirect their activities *before* they start to misbehave. You can go for some food, watch a video, or take them to the park. We wanted to have positive experiences follow positive behaviors. Instead of waiting for trouble, we would rechannel their attention while they were doing well.

"When the boys got older, we became even more proactive about what we wanted and needed them to do. We set goals with them in areas like helping around the house, doing well in school, taking care of their rooms, and getting along with adults and friends. We'd watch them closely, and when they did well, we'd praise them. When they didn't do something they were supposed to do, rather than spending a lot of time on that, we'd go back to the goals we'd agreed upon and get them refocused on them. Our kids have grown up in an environment where they know good things happen when they are 'taking care of business.'

"Sometimes we'd hear our friends making comparisons between their kids," Dave continued. 'Sally does so well at everything, but Betsy never seems to do things quite right. I wish she were more like her sister.' In observing how they treated their girls, it didn't take a great deal of insight to figure out what was happening. The parents were using a WHALE DONE approach with Sally, but Betsy was caught in the GOTcha game. When we suggested to our friends that they accentuate the positive with Betsy, their response was quick: 'But she isn't doing anything that deserves our praise.' See, these parents were in a perceptual trap. The only way out was to start to observe Betsy doing some things just a little bit better. If her room looked even slightly neater today than yesterday, she deserved a WHALE DONE for that. They needed to cheerlead her progress.

"Unfortunately when kids get off on the wrong foot they often learn that the only way they can get their parents' attention, compared to their do-good sibling, is to act out. Unless you're playing WHALE DONE with *all* your kids, things can get out of balance. Redirecting and giving 'approximately right' WHALE DONEs are the keys to turning poor behavior around. Meanwhile, if you continue to recognize good behavior, this program can go a long way to building happy families."

"It's certainly worth a try," Joy said.

"Humans naturally want approval from others," Dave went on. "When you're dealing with your kids or with the people at work, and you consistently call attention to what they do right, it's like you're responding to the best that's in them. After a while, they begin to enjoy all the positive attention. They find out it's more fun to succeed and achieve and be praised for it."

Just then the girls returned with Pam. "Mom! Dad! This place is so cool! Thanks for bringing us here!" exclaimed Allie.

After the family said their thank-yous and good-byes to Dave and Pam, they walked past the edge of Shamu's pool. The huge whale swam over to them. "Good-bye, Shamu," Meg said, blowing him a kiss. "You sure are a good teacher!"

 Chapter Five

Upon their return from Florida, Wes and Joy lost no time in convening a family meeting. Its purpose was to begin to replace some of their previous ways of parenting with WHALE DONE methods. Joy made sure to prepare several of Meg and Allie's favorite foods for dinner that evening, and the four of them gathered in the living room afterward for dessert.

Wes started things off. "Your mom and I are very thankful that you girls could be at SeaWorld with us and find out, as we did, how they train the killer whales. From what you've said, Pam told you about the WHALE DONE methods the trainers use. What did you learn that was unusual?"

Meg began with a bright and hopeful expression. "I liked the idea of paying attention to the good things the whales do, instead of how they're naughty."

"If you focus on the actions you want," said Allie, "you get more of them."

"That's exactly right," Wes said. "Do you think it would be a good idea to try to use the WHALE DONE methods around here? Mom and I are not too proud about how we've been acting toward you. We've paid a lot more attention to the times when you've goofed up than to the times when you've done what we asked you to do."

"We've noticed," Allie replied with a frown.

"Okay, we're guilty as charged," Joy said. "We want to do better, but to change things around, we first need to make some agreements. Then we can give each other WHALE DONEs whenever we keep them."

"I'll agree to keep my room picked up," Meg said. "I'm tired of getting yelled at."

"Me, too," Allie added. "And I'll tidy up the kitchen after I have friends over for a snack."

"That would be great," Joy said. "Daddy and I will be looking for ways to give you WHALE DONEs for any improvements you make around the house."

"And as a reward," Wes said, "why don't we agree that whoever helps prepare a meal and sets the table doesn't have to clean up afterwards?"

"I'd love *that!*" said Joy.

"Does that mean Meg and I can fix dinner sometimes?" asked Allie.

"Sure. Then Mom and I will have to do the cleanup."

"Another thing," Joy said, "I dread Saturday mornings around here. The house goes through some wear and tear during the week, and there's a lot of cleaning up to do. I usually end up doing it all myself, and I'd like some help."

"Why don't we do like in *Snow White*?" Meg put in brightly. "We could all take an hour every Saturday morning and be dwarfs!"

"Could we whistle while we work?" Allie said patronizingly.

"Maybe you'd like to be Grumpy," Mom added with a smile.

Allie laughed and said, "Any chance of getting Mary Poppins to show up and whisk all the mess away?"

"I'm afraid not," Joy said. "But there's a pretty good chance we could go to the mall or think up some other activity you'd like to do after the job is done."

The meeting ended when the girls went upstairs to do their homework without being told. "You know," Joy said, sinking back into the couch contentedly, "I like this WHALE DONE business already."

"Maybe we need a WHALE DONE makeover in our own relationship," Wes suggested a few nights later.

"I agree," Joy said. "I certainly learned in our discussion with Dave that I was playing the GOTcha game with you."

Wes smiled. "I haven't exactly been accentuating the positive with you, either."

"Why don't we give Anne Marie Butler a call?" Joy said. "You've been talking so much about what you learned from her that I'd like to meet her, even if it's over the phone. Maybe she can help us get started on improving our relationship."

Wes agreed and dialed the beeper number Anne Marie had given him. Within minutes the phone rang and Wes put it on the speaker mode. "Hi, Wes!" Anne Marie's cheerful voice seemed to fill the room. "What's up?"

"I want you to meet my best friend," Wes said. "Say hello to Joy."

"Hi, Joy. Glad to meet you. Wes has told me a lot about you."

"Hi, Anne Marie," Joy said. "Wes and I have been discussing our goals for our own WHALE DONE relationship, and we thought you might have some ideas for us. We both have to admit that in recent years we've fallen into a GOTcha pattern."

"That certainly can happen in any relationship," Anne Marie said. "I can't say enough about the power of WHALE DONE to energize and enhance a marriage. Let me start by telling you something that happened recently when my husband and I were having dinner at a fancy French restaurant. We noticed two couples at nearby tables. On one side was a couple who were obviously in love. When one of them was speaking, what do you think the other one was doing? Listening. Smiling. Patting the other's hand. Giving undivided attention. It probably took them two and a half hours to eat, but I don't think they would have complained if they'd never been served any food."

"On the other side was another couple who were obviously bored to death. They had nothing to say. They didn't even look at each other. They acted as if the only reason they were there together was because they couldn't get anybody else to eat with them. 'That marriage is dead,' I said to my husband, 'but nobody's bothered to bury it.' "

"I think we've seen a few of those relationships, ourselves," Wes said.

"How do you get from the edge of your seat to having nothing to say?" Anne Marie asked. "It's the frequency with which you catch each other doing something right. Did you ever hear the saying 'Love is blind'?"

"Sure," said Joy.

"What does that mean?"

"It means," Wes said, "that when you first fall in love, all you see is the positive."

"That's right," Anne Marie agreed. "So when you start a love relationship, the emphasis is completely on the positive; you don't notice anything negative—or disregard it as unimportant. It's not until you get married and move in together that you start to notice all those things in your partner to which your love was blind in the beginning. Pretty soon, *those* behaviors are what you focus on. Even if your partner attempts to change, you don't notice or acknowledge the progress. You start yelling at each other, even for little things. The final demise of a love relationship is when you do something *right* and you still get yelled at because you didn't do it right *enough!* 'You had to *ask* me!' . . . 'You should have done it on *Wednesday!*' "

"This is getting painfully familiar," Joy said.

"It's a very common pattern," Anne Marie continued. "People ask me all the time if I do marriage counseling. I tell them, 'No, but I'll ask you one question. It's the same question you should ask yourself, not only about your love relationship but about your relationship with your kids, your boss, the people who report to you, your colleagues, and your friends. The question is, do you want the relationship to work?" She paused. "How about you two?"

"We certainly want to give it a try," Wes said.

"Trying is just a noisier way of not doing something," Anne Marie came back. "I run into people all the time who are going to marriage counseling. When I ask them why, they say, 'We're trying to make our relationship work.' I tell them to save their money. Marriage counseling is never successful unless both parties are committed to making the relationship work. If one or both mates are hedging their bets—in other words, 'trying'—no one will be honest because the relationship is still on trial.

"Once a commitment is made to the relationship, now you can take on any problem or issue without fear that something you say will end it all. You are both *committed to your commitment*. So let me ask again, Wes. Do you want your relationship with Joy to work?"

"Yes!" Wes answered emphatically.

"How about you, Joy? Do you want to make your relationship with Wes work?"

Joy took a moment to reply. "I'll have to admit that for a while before we went to Florida I wasn't sure. But after talking to Dave, and now to you, I'm beginning to understand about the negative cycle we'd gotten ourselves into." Joy squeezed Wes's hand as she added, "That's why I'm ready to say yes to your question about commitment."

"I've got to hand it to you two," Anne Marie said. "With both of you agreed on your commitment to each other, you've got a great foundation for success. Of course, you know it's going to take work."

"Oh, we know it!" both Joy and Wes agreed.

"I also think it's a good idea to sit down and renew your commitment periodically," said Anne Marie. "Like anything that fades with neglect, it needs occasional refurbishing."

Then Joy said, "I bet I know what you're going to say next."

"What's that?"

"That once you make a commitment to your commitment, the plan is to start to enjoy playing WHALE DONE with one another, and if you do that, you'll probably have a lot of fun noticing all the new things you're both doing to improve your relationship."

"You took the words right out of my mouth," Anne Marie said. "Actually, that's just following the law of positive-to-positive. Positive responses motivate people to continue to do positive things. It's an upward spiral."

"For curiosity's sake," said Wes, "what if a couple's answer to the commitment question is no?"

"Then I would suggest they go to marriage counseling to get help on how they can separate without beating up each other or the kids. It's possible to develop a plan to end a relationship in a positive way."

"Well, we're looking to accentuate the positive, aren't we, Joy?"

"Right. Any suggestions, Anne Marie, for how to get started?"

"Why don't you sit down together and think about a couple of problems you seem to be having in your relationship. Then discuss the positive ways you can go about solving them."

Wes and Joy took Anne Marie's advice. They sat down that very evening and began to talk honestly about their needs. Joy set the WHALE DONE tone right away by telling Wes that she loved having him home in the evening when they could all be together as a family. "That's why I've been so negative," she confided. "When you never seemed to be around, it hurt, and I started up the GOTcha game."

"What would it be like," Wes asked, "if I stopped coming home late?"

Joy's eyes widened. "To me it would mean that at least a couple of nights a week I would know that our family came first. I know that your work is important to you and it's going to take some real effort. But it should bring us together as a family, not keep us apart. Your coming home to dinner on time should be the rule rather than the exception."

"I agree with you," Wes said. "Our family should come first. You know there will probably be some crunch periods when I have to work late hours, but I'm definitely going to start this week coming home on time. Not only that, I'm going to leave the work behind—the tasks *and* the worries."

"And I'll stop nagging you about every little thing you do wrong so you'll *want* to come home," Joy said. "Nobody's perfect. But now that I think about it, you deserve a lot of WHALE DONEs for all the good things you do for me and the girls."

"Music to my ears." Wes gave Joy a kiss.

A few days later, Allie spoke to her mother about a friend. "Maureen has been talking to me about her boyfriend, Hugh. She's upset because he's started hanging around with some questionable characters. Maureen would like to spend more time with him, but she's worried that Hugh will get into trouble. She told me his folks recently went through a divorce. Hugh misses his dad, and his mother is always criticizing him. Maureen knows he's just being rebellious because of the family situation. You're friends with Hugh's mom. Do you think you could talk to her?"

"I know his mother's been having trouble adjusting to being a single working mom ever since she and her husband split up," Joy said. "And she's told me Hugh's been a handful. I'm concerned, too, Allie, but I don't want to pry. Parents can't tell other parents what to do with their kids."

"I know, Mom." Allie said. "But maybe you could just ask her out for coffee and a chat. It would mean a lot to Maureen."

Joy thought about her daughter's request for several days. Hugh's mother, Sharon, wasn't the first person to whom she wished she could impart the principles of WHALE DONE parenting. Finally she phoned her friend and they made a date to meet the following morning for an early coffee before going to work.

"Oh, boy!" Sharon said with a huge sigh when they met. "Nobody told me it was going to be this hard. Full working days at a new job, plus constant worries about a teenager who's driving me crazy!"

Sharon began to pour out her troubles about Hugh, and Joy quickly realized that out of fear and frustration

Sharon was developing a classic GOTcha game with her son. "I've told him repeatedly that I want him to let me know where he's going and who he's with, but does he? No way! You'd think he could at least leave me a note. Is it too much to ask that he just call home?"

While Joy sympathized with her friend, she saw clearly that Sharon was worsening her relationship with Hugh by focusing on the things he was doing wrong. After sitting patiently through a laundry list of grievances, Joy finally said, "I know it's got to be really hard working all day, not knowing where Hugh is or if he's going to be okay. I know you love him, and this is a tough time for both of you. But it's also a time when you and Hugh have to be friends, not enemies. I have a couple of suggestions that seem to be working wonders with my own girls. Would you like to hear them?"

"Anything," Sharon begged. "I'm at my wit's end."

By the time their conversation ended, Sharon had made two lists for herself. The first was of ways to convey her needs to Hugh without blame and to set up reasonable agreements with him. The second was of ways she could begin catching Hugh doing things right when he lived up to his agreements or improved even in the slightest. Sharon's eyes were shining as she hugged Joy. "Thank you!" she said with deep feeling. "I'd begun to forget what hope feels like."

 Chapter Six

ONE DAY AT THE OFFICE Wes was coaching an account representative through a problem when his boss approached him. "Could I see you a minute?" a grim-faced Jim Barnes asked. The two men walked back to Barnes's office, where he closed the door and said, "Have a seat." After they were settled, Barnes said, "I guess you know that your latest sales figures are dropping. Any reason I should know about?"

Wes was taken aback, but he was aware of the problem. "The Minnesota account, which has always been big, has slowed its orders the past three months, but I think that will pick up. Also I've had some shifts in personnel. I'm training new people and it's taking time to get them up to speed."

"I know about all that," Barnes said dismissively. "The fact is you're not getting the sales you used to get from your people. They weren't great fans of yours, but you could always punch up their productivity. I think the problem is that you've grown soft."

"Soft?"

Barnes reached into his pocket and held up one of the tiny WHALE DONE toy whales that Wes had been giving out. "This, for instance," he said in disgust. "You've got your people playing with toys."

"Those are tokens of encouragement. It's all part of—"

"And I've heard about some of the new language you're using!" Barnes interrupted. "GOTcha? WHALE DONE? What's that all about?"

Whoops! I was afraid of something like this! Wes thought to himself, but he said, "Not to worry, Jim. It's a new management technique. It's well researched, and it will work."

Barnes got up abruptly and strode around the room. "Some research! It was developed for training *whales*, for God's sake!"

"That's true. But the technique is simple and basic. It's all about responding positively instead of negatively to someone's performance. I used to jump all over my people when they made a mistake and just take it for granted when they did something right. Now I'm getting along much better with all of them."

"That's not what I've heard," Barnes grumbled.

"What have you heard? Don't leave me in the dark, Jim. Did somebody come to you?"

Barnes shook his head in annoyance. "No names," he finally said. "But in the past week I've heard from two people who think you've lost your edge with the team. From what they told me, it sounds like the patients are running the hospital."

"That's ridiculous, Jim. Just because I'm trying to take the pressure off—"

"That's the trouble, right there," Barnes came back, jabbing a finger at Wes. "This is no time to take the pressure off. It's time to put it *on*. Look, Wes, I don't care how you do it, but get those sales figures up. Bill Jaspers was riding me this morning about the overall performance of our department, and he wants those numbers changed. Do whatever you have to do."

"Okay, I hear you. Loud and clear."

"Another thing. Do I need to remind you that our performance review is coming up in April? You know what that means. No matter how much kindness you show your people, you can't give them all an excellent rating. You and I know how the system works. The normal distribution curve is a fact of life around here. Your job is to separate the excellent performers from the average ones, and the average ones from the poor ones. We're not running a country club."

As Wes left Barnes's office and started down the hall, he saw Harvey Meehan and Gus Sulermo duck into Gus's office. He was pretty sure now who the two "people" were who'd gone to his boss behind his back.

Later that afternoon, when he knew that Harvey and Gus were together in the break room, Wes went to see them. "Hi, guys. Got a minute? I wonder if you can help me? I see you two as leaders on our team, and your influence on the others is important. Sales are down, and we can bring them back up if we don't work at odds with each other."

"GOTcha!" Harvey said.

Ignoring the slur, Wes went on, "I'm proposing a deal. For the next six months, I need you guys to cooperate and get behind the changes I'm trying to make around here—and also to take it easy and not be so quick to shoot down my management style. If our results and our relationships are no better after that time, I'll agree to stop pushing WHALE DONE. What do you say?"

The pair looked dubiously at each other, then reluctantly nodded their agreement. Wes had the impression they did so because their shared business goals were at stake, so he said with enthusiasm, "Thanks, guys. I imagine saying yes to my request is not particularly enjoyable for you, yet you did it without hesitation.

I admire that." He walked away, aware of the pair's stunned silence. But as he went back to his office, he found himself wondering whether the techniques Dave Yardley used with killer whales could really work in business.

The night after Wes's meeting with his boss, he and Joy were talking about the strides she and the girls were making. She was delighted with the number of opportunities she was finding to praise their progress around the goals the family had set. "Do you think this WHALE DONE business is getting any easier?" she asked Wes.

"I definitely think it is." Then he added, "For *you!*"

"Why? What's bothering you?"

Wes sighed. "I agree that WHALE DONE is working here at home, but the office is a different story. I had a disconcerting meeting with Jim Barnes today. He thinks our unit's troubles are due to the fact that I've got whales on the brain. He thinks I've gone soft and he wants me to put back the pressure on my unit."

"I'm sorry to hear that."

"When organizations are under pressure, the first things to be abandoned are experimental management approaches. It's back to my-way-or-the-highway, yet I've already proved that doesn't work. This crunch has people worried about losing their jobs. Frankly, the way Jim looked at me today, I thought, 'Maybe I'll be the first to go.' "

The next morning Wes called Anne Marie Butler to give her his periodic update. When she asked him how things were going, he said, "Which do you want first, the good news or the bad news?"

"You know me, let's hear the good news."

"Okay, I'll start with Joy's and my relationship. I'm happy to say that catching each other doing things right has almost become a habit. It's always a little surprising, though—especially when one of us voices appreciation of the other in front of the kids."

"How do you mean?"

"The other night at dinner Joy said to me, 'Honey, thanks for calling and telling me you'd be a little late. I was able to hold off final preparations for dinner so we could wait for you and all eat together. I like that much better.'

"Then Allie chimed in, 'Mom, you never used to brag about Dad.'

"Joy said, 'You're right. Do you think I'm bragging about him because he's getting better?'

"You'll appreciate Allie's reply. She said, 'No. He's getting better because you're bragging about him.' "

"That makes perfect sense to me," Anne Marie said.

"Allie's right," Wes went on. "Since Joy and I have been playing the WHALE DONE game, our mutual love and respect has deepened until it's no longer a game at all. It's become the way we look at each other. We're more affectionate and wanting to spend more time together. The girls have noticed that, too. The other day Allie remarked, 'You guys sure are mushy lately.'

" 'Yeah,' Meg said. 'You're always hugging and holding hands.'

" 'Does that make you uncomfortable?' Joy asked them.

" 'Not really,' Allie answered. 'We thought it was funny at first, but we've gotten used to it.'

" 'It feels cozy to me,' Meg said.

" 'How so?' I asked.

" 'Well, when I see you loving each other, I feel more loved.' Joy and I just beamed at each other.

"Then Allie said, 'As usual, Meg's right. I guess in a way I feel proud that my parents actually show that they love each other. Some of my friends' parents don't seem even to *like* each other that much.' "

"It seems like you and Joy are becoming a 'catching couple'!" Anne Marie said. "What else is happening?"

"I'm kind of amazed at the way my relationship with Allie has improved. The other day she said to me, 'I looked around in your closet, Dad, but I couldn't find your costume.' Knowing I was being baited, I asked her, 'Okay, what costume?' 'Your Super-Dad suit!' she said." Wes chuckled and added, "I think she *likes* me!"

"Of course she does," Anne Marie said. "Why do you think she's changed?"

"Because Joy and I have been giving both of the girls a lot of WHALE DONEs lately. And they deserve them!"

"I think," Anne Marie said, "there's an even more fundamental reason for Allie's change in attitude."

"Like what?" Wes asked.

"Do me a favor. Put your right hand on your left shoulder, and your left hand on your right shoulder. Then give yourself a big hug. You've changed, too, Wes. You're a different person than when I first met you."

"Well, thanks. I don't want to get a big head."

"As long as you're busy accentuating the positive with others, a little self-praise won't hurt," Anne Marie said. "I come across a lot of managers who are hard on others because they're so hard on themselves. They're always after themselves in their heads. 'Oh, I should have done that better,' or, 'What a dummy I am, forgetting that detail.' Sound like anybody you know?"

"*Ohhh* yeah!" Wes said, laughing.

"If you catch *yourself* doing things right, everything in your life will improve—especially your relationships. That's because it's fun to be around someone who likes himself."

"Is that your secret?" Wes asked.

"Maybe. As my father always told me . . .

It never hurts to toot your own horn once in a while.

"I guess now's the time for the bad news, Anne Marie."

"Bring it on."

Wes told Anne Marie about the meeting with his boss the previous day, including Barnes's warning about the performance review and the necessity to rate his people on a normal distribution curve. Wes also described his confrontation with Harvey and Gus.

"Let's talk about the resisters first," Anne Marie said. "My advice to you is hang in there! People will doubt and people will obstruct. A certain amount of that may even be necessary. What I've found is that very often the people who oppose change are just cautious in the beginning. But once they buy in, they become your biggest supporters. Trust your people. Stick to your guns, and keep your boss informed. WHALE DONE will work."

"Thanks, I hope so."

"Now, as for the performance review system your company is using, that's a problem. In my travels I often ask audiences, 'How many of you think the way you receive feedback and the way your performance is evaluated is important to you?' Every hand in the place goes up. Then I ask them, 'How many of you are thrilled with the way you presently receive feedback and have your performance evaluated?' Almost no hands ever go up—just a few people from personnel, who probably developed the system.

"Why don't people like their performance review system?" Anne Marie continued. "Because it forces managers like you to sort them out into top, average, and poor performances—regardless of where they really fit."

"That certainly describes how our company's system

works," said Wes. "It makes it hard to implement WHALE DONE, doesn't it?"

"It sure does. The toughest situation is when all of your people are excellent. *Now* who are you going to rate average or poor? That kind of performance review sets people up to compete with each other. It eliminates cooperation and team spirit. I ask top managers, 'How many of you, thinking of evaluation time, say, 'Let's go out and hire some losers so we can fill some of our low slots?' They laugh and I say, 'Of course you don't. You either hire winners or potential winners—people you think will perform well when they're trained and encouraged. In other words . . .

**If you don't hire people
on a performance review curve,
why grade them on one?**

Wes understood how the traditional view of evaluating performance was at odds with the WHALE DONE philosophy, but he was uncertain what it implied for him. "What are you suggesting I do?"

"Your boss is putting pressure on you to turn the numbers around. Why don't you share with your people that, as part of WHALE DONE management, you're not going to use the old performance review system that forces managers to sort people out into excellent, average, and poor performers? Tell them that WHALE DONE implies the opposite—i.e., that everyone has the opportunity to win. It will encourage people to compete against themselves—their own capacity to accomplish their goals—and not against each other. Show them that their wins shouldn't be considered others' potential losses."

"How am I going to promise that?" Wes asked. "Barnes and the others would take my head off."

"I realize it's going out on a limb, but you have to trust that if you and your people really get with it and cheer each other on in a noncompetitive way, your numbers will speak for themselves. That's all Barnes and his boss are really concerned about, anyway. Then when you turn in your performance evaluations, you should have no poor performers. That is, unless you've got somebody who's in the wrong job. If someone, no matter how they're trained and encouraged, is not able to perform up to standard, they shouldn't be punished. They should be shifted to a position where they can succeed."

"Okay. I'll do it. Thanks, Anne Marie. Life certainly has become an adventure since I met Dave, Shamu, and you."

Wes hung up the phone, then sat at his desk in deep thought. While he appreciated his friend's help and boundless energy, he still felt somewhat lost. His mind was full of questions. Should he keep on applying WHALE DONE at work? Might it not endanger his future with the company? Could he really convince his boss to change the evaluation system, even if all his people were performing well?

That night Wes couldn't sleep. A blackness had descended on his spirit that he couldn't shake. Before dawn he dressed and left for the office. As he drove through the deserted streets, his mood deepened. *I'm getting sabotaged from the top,* he thought to himself. *Anne Marie's idea of my changing the performance evaluation system on my own is crazy. I'm ready to bail.*

Entering his company's office, Wes stood for a moment at the door to the meeting room where he had made his kickoff speech to the team about WHALE DONE and explained how he planned to use it. He shook his head. Had it all been a disaster from the start?

Just then he heard a key turning in the outside door. Someone else was coming into work early. It was Merideth, and when she saw him, she said, "Boy, you're an early bird." Then, noting his hangdog expression, she asked, "Is something the matter?"

"Everything's fine." How could he tell her he had come in early to work on his résumé, or that he was thinking about a letter of resignation?

"Well," said Merideth, "things are tough, but here's a news flash. If you're about to abandon ship on the WHALE DONE program, don't even think about it. Your praise and encouragement are about the only bright spots around here—except for the times I find myself and the other supervisors copying you and cheering our people on, too. I know this doesn't sound like me, but I mean it." She took off down the hall, obviously eager to get to work.

Wes felt a surge of energy. Anne Marie's encouragement, together with Merideth's attaboy, had tipped the scales, and once again he was sure that WHALE DONE was the way to go. Abandoning his thoughts of giving up, he resolved to keep his commitment to his commitment.

"Let's get started," said Wes as his monthly sales meeting came to order. Gesturing to a young man seated to his right, he said, "I'd like you all to meet Howard

LaRosse, who will be heading up our telemarketing sales. This is Howie's first day. He hasn't even been through our orientation program, but I thought it wouldn't hurt for him to sit in on our meeting today."

As applause broke out, the expression on Howie's face showed that he hadn't expected such a warm welcome.

"As most of you know," Wes continued, "we start the meeting by catching each other doing things right. Who'd like to go first?"

"I'll go," said tall, sandy-haired Marsha. "My sales goal for this month was two hundred thousand. I achieved ninety-two percent of it."

Sincere applause greeted Marsha's announcement. She was followed by Lyle, who reported that he had hit 110 percent of his goal. Roberto said he had achieved 72 percent of his goal. As more salespeople continued to share their figures, each report was met with another round of applause.

Next, Wes asked for comments or questions.

Howie raised his hand. "I'm the rookie here, so I need help understanding this process. In other companies I've worked for, the only applause would have been for people who had met or exceeded their goals. Here, you seem to be praising any progress that's made at all. I guess if I showed that kind of acceptance with my team, I'd be afraid that it might take away from their desire to improve."

Wes asked, "Who'd like to respond to Howie's concern?" A few hands went up, and Wes gave the nod to Pete, one of the veteran salespeople who reported to him.

"That's the way things used to be around here, too," Pete said, "until recently. Now we're practicing what we call the WHALE DONE method. It always seems to start things off right. Because we accentuate the positive, no one hangs back from sharing their performance record, and even their problems. As you'll see, during the next part of the meeting we'll brainstorm ideas to help each other improve. Each of us can tap into the brainpower of the whole group."

"I get it," Howie said. "This way there's none of the internal competition you usually see on teams."

"Right," Pete said, "WHALE DONE has us competing with ourselves, rather than each other."

Over the succeeding months, the new approach to managing performance began to catch on with other units, and Wes found himself in demand as a consultant. Merideth and some other supervisors even prepared a presentation based on WHALE DONE success stories and took it to other departments. In time, the shift in the way people felt they were being treated proved to be the turnaround for the company. Gradually everyone's sales began to increase. For Wes, the ultimate sign that things had changed occurred the day he was in his office preparing for a meeting with Jim Barnes to review the current sales figures. A knock sounded and he looked up to see Harvey and Gus standing there.

"Can we see you for a few minutes?" Harvey asked.

"Of course. I'm always glad to talk with you," Wes said, "even if you still have some kind of ax to grind!"

"That's what we want to see you about," Harvey said. "Is it okay to come in?"

Wes motioned them to chairs.

Harvey began, "We know you've been trying hard to turn things around, going out of your way to support everybody, and we've been obstructing you. We're just here to tell you that we're not in your way anymore."

"We want to help," Gus said, finding his voice.

"That's good news, guys," Wes said, "and I've got some good news to share with you. All of the sales figures are up. Several people—including both of you—have been outstanding, but everyone here has been performing consistently above the standard. I'm about to meet with Jim Barnes to go over our quarterly report, and I'm going to tell him how important accentuating the positive has been to our unit's success. Everyone has improved. There are no losers, and I intend to insist that the present performance review system that forces managers to grade people into high, average, and poor groups shouldn't apply to our team."

Harvey's and Gus's enthusiastic reactions gave Wes an idea. Why not take the two of them with him to meet with his boss? A three-on-one fast break would be tough for Jim Barnes to defend.

It was. Barnes couldn't argue with the performance of Wes's unit or the support Harvey and Gus were now giving his management approach. That meeting ended with Barnes promising to take the performance review battle to his boss. Wes never forgot the smile on his boss's face as he said, "WHALE DONE, Wes!"

As succeeding months went by and the WHALE DONE approach was in high gear at the Kingsley household, Wes and Joy began to notice that, in addition to the improvements in their family relationships, there were other benefits as well. Allie's and Meg's friends, drawn to the accepting atmosphere they found there, were beginning to spend more and more time at their house. On weekends, Joy, an adept pianist, was in demand by teenagers to accompany impromptu sing-alongs and parties. Sometimes there were messes after the get-togethers, and Joy and Wes made agreements with the kids about the cleanup. When it was time to go home, the youngsters would count off and form teams, then race each other to see how quickly they could restore the house to immaculate order.

When difficulties arose, Wes and Joy were glad they'd been careful to develop relationships not only with each of their daughters' friends, but with their parents, as well. They kept an eye on some of them whose influence might be questionable. Allie's friends found ready listeners in both Wes and Joy, and many of them confided things in them they would not tell their own parents. The Kingsleys knew they had truly made their home a welcome place when they began to receive calls from parents who wondered, "How come my kids are always over at your house?"

Whenever Joy and Wes talked about the many positive changes in their lives, they said, "What would everybody think if they knew it was all because of a whale?"

 Epilogue

IT WAS SEPTEMBER, a year or so later, and Wes was again in Orlando on business. He was drawn back to SeaWorld to visit the place where his life had begun to change for the better, and to touch base with his old friends Shamu and Dave Yardley. As usual, before going to see Dave, he had stopped by the stadium to watch the killer whale show. As the huge, sleek animals went through their paces, some of which were new to him, Wes whooped and applauded with the rest of the crowd.

Now as the show ended and people began to filter out, he heard the young man sitting in the seat next to him say to his family, "Gee, how do you suppose they get those whales to do all that?"

Wes smiled and drew a deep breath. "Funny you should ask," he said to the man.

Acknowledgments

THIS BOOK HAS BEEN more than ten years in the making. Along the journey, a number of people have helped us in important ways. We begin with special grateful and hearty WHALE DONEs to two key people: Margret McBride, our esteemed literary agent, for always believing in us and for making this book better with her ideas. And Fred Hills, gentlemanly editor at The Free Press, for his eagle eye on the manuscript and for his skillful practice of the art of teaming with authors.

In addition, we'd all like to acknowledge Paul Hersey, Spencer Johnson, Robert Lorber, and Norman Vincent Peale, former coauthors with Ken, and David Berlo and Aubrey Daniels, behavioral scientists *extraordinaire*, for influencing his thinking and many of the concepts presented in this book. Also, our friends at the Skaneateles Country Club, who reviewed the manuscript and provided invaluable feedback.

Ken: I want to acknowledge Eleanor Terndrup, Dana Kyle, and Dottie Hamilt, who at different times over the many years of my thinking about this book have been my right hand. And most especially to my wife, Margie, who is always in my corner.

Thad: I want to acknowledge my family—Barbara, Michelle, and Philip—for their consistent support and love. Chuck and I also wish to give WHALE DONEs to Ted Turner, Mike Scarpuzzi, and Dave Force for their positive professional influence and, most importantly, for their friendship.

Chuck: I want to thank my wife, Kathy, and my two sons, Cody and Jared, for their encouragement, patience, and love, and for being the real inspiration for this book.

Jim: To my best friend, personal editor, and "light bulb," Barbara Perman, whose ideas have influenced this writing so deeply; to fellow author Jayne Pearl for her help; and to Matt and the gang down at Collective Copies.

WHALE DONE, everybody!

About the Authors

Ken Blanchard is Chief Spiritual Officer and Chairman of the Board of the Ken Blanchard Companies. He is the author of a dozen best-selling books—including the blockbuster international best-seller *The One Minute Manager* and the giant business best-sellers *Raving Fans* and *Gung Ho!*—which have combined sales of more than 12 million copies in more than twenty-five languages. He is married with two children and lives in San Diego, California.

Thad Lacinak is vice president and nationwide director of animal training for Busch Entertainment Corporation, with more than twenty-eight years of experience in marine mammal training. Married and the father of two children, he lives in Windermere, Florida.

Chuck Tompkins is vice president and head of animal training at SeaWorld in Orlando, Florida. Married and the father of two children, he lives in Orlando, Florida.

Jim Ballard is an educator, corporate trainer, and writer and has worked closely on three books with Ken Blanchard, *Mission Possible, Everyone's a Coach*, and *Managing by Values*. Jim has four children and lives in Amherst, Massachusetts.

Services Available

Ken Blanchard speaks to conventions and organizations all over the world, and The Ken Blanchard Companies, a full-service management and consulting training company, conducts seminars and in-depth consulting in the areas of teamwork, customer service, leadership, performance management, and quality.

All four of the *WHALE DONE!* authors are available to make presentations and conduct seminars. To make arrangements, contact:

The Ken Blanchard Companies
125 State Place
Escondido, CA 92029
800/728-6000 or 760/489-5005
760/489-8407 (Fax)

Visit us on our Web Site:
www.kenblanchard.com